of his documentations; unfortunatel
scholarly arguments and hasten to the bottom line--which is that the Dead Sea Scrolls and the Nag Hammadi texts <u>do</u> indeed support Mormon claims to possess genuine beliefs restored from the time of the ancient Church.

Incidentally, it would behoove Norman Geisler--who supplied the foreword to Ms. Layton's booklet--to avoid placing too much confidence in the Tanners' <u>Mormonism: Shadow</u> or <u>Reality?,</u> for those who live by such books are likely to perish by them as well. I refer to the endless shelves of "debunking" literature in the shops and libraries condemning Catholicism, Anglicanism, Seventh Day Adventism, Jehovah's Witnesses, Calvinism, Lutheranism, or even Christianity in general, with exactly the same sort of historical contradictions and human foibles that are used against the Mormons. Mormons are admittedly no less susceptible to human weakness than the Inquisitors, the Borgia Popes, Henry VIII, Martin Luther, William Miller, Judge Rutherford, Colonel Kellogg, and a host of others, whose very names are infamous to many; but this does not constitute any rational disproof of their beliefs or evidence that God has not offered them a way to improve themselves.

We would rather challenge the reader to explain just how Joseph Smith was able to incorporate so many of antiquity's forgotten doctrines into Mormonism, preserving at the same time the authentic patterns in which they originally appeared. Even if one desired to reject these doctrines, one would be hard-pressed to account for the fact that he knew of their existence, and at a time and place where nothing of the sort had been previously suspected. This remarkable fact should be pondered by all who question the relationship of Mormonism to the texts from the Dead Sea and the Egyptian desert.

-GLOSSARY-

ACHAMOTH--A Gnostic name for Sophia (q.v.), derived from the Hebrew word chochmah, "Wisdom".

APOCALYPTIC--A movement common to early Christianity and Judaism, revealing the hidden secrets of God's transcendent Kingdom and the approaching eschaton (q, v.)

BENE ELOHIM--(Bene ha-elohim), Hebrew, "sons of God", the members of the ancient pantheon; became the "angels" of monotheism.

BRIDAL CHAMBER--The Holy of Holies in the Jerusalem Temple; anciently, the entire area behind the veil (= "Celestial Room").

CARPOCRATIANS--A Gnostic sect which incorporated reincarnation doctrine, possibly from Pythagorean or Indian sources.

DAMASCUS COVENANTERS--An Essence sect which had settled near Damascus to escape persecution. They were related to the Qumran sect, and their Damascus Document is now included among the "Dead Sea Scrolls".

DEMIURGE--Greek for "artificer", The Gnostic version of the OT Creator, who was looked down upon because he was the Author of the material world, and because he was the "arrogant" God of the Jews, who considered himself to be the "only" God. Evidence that early Christians were acquainted with the existence of a God other than the OT Yahweh (v. the Unknown Father).

DOCETISM--The late Gnostic doctrine that Jesus only appeared to possess a material body, which was actually composed of spirit, the true reality.

DUAL PATERNITY--The doctrine that every person has two fathers, the human father and the Heavenly Father of the spirit.

ESCHATON, ESCHATOLOGICAL--Greek for "End", i.e. the Last Days, "Eschatological" refers to that which is destined to appear at the end of time, "Eschatological pre-existence" refers to that which already exists in heaven, awaiting the Last Days, when it will became manifest.

ESSENES--A branch of apocalyptic Judaism emphasizing avoidance of worldliness, ritual purity, the transcendent nature of the soul, and the imminent coming of God's messianic Kingdom. The Qumran Community is generally considered to be a branch of Essenism, and a source of certain ideas embraced by Primitive Christianity.

GNOSIS--Greek for "knowledge", esp., secret knowledge of man's true nature, making possible escape from material existence. Gnosis was the broad basis for Gnosticism (q.v.), its specifically Christian form. Gnosis was common to Primitive Christianity, heterodox Judaism, Mandaeism, Manichaeism, and other contemporary philosophies of the age.

GNOSTICISM--Traditionally supposed to be a heretical departure from "orthodox" Christianity. Now recognized as an indigenous development of certain tendencies within Christianity itself, emphasizing man's divine origin, pre-existence and

4

"exile" in the material world. Salvation is achieved when the Redeemer defeats the "powers" that bind man to the elements, bringing him the saving Gnosis (q.v.) of his true nature which makes it possible for him to be led back to his heavenly home. Gnosticism eventually developed a fanatical hatred for everything physical, and a one-sided veneration for the purely spiritual.

HEXAMERON SPECULATION--From Greek hexaemera, the "six days" (of Creation), meaning the spiritual creation of the pre-existent Church. A secret doctrine of the Primitive Christians.

HIEROS GAMOS--Greek for "Sacred Marriage", i.e. ritual or archetypal copulation representing the divine union of the sexes, after which human marriage is patterned. It was also allegorized to represent the spiritual union of Yahweh and Israel, or Christ and the Church.

LIMBS OF THE LOVER--Jewish expression for the vision of God on his Throne, the object of mystical union, as allegorized in Song of Songs.

NAASSENES--A branch of Gnosticism, named after nahas (Hebrew, "serpent"), the bringer of knowledge to Adam and Eve.

PLEROMA--In Gnosticism, the heavenly Community of Light, in which the spirits of men were first begotten; also called the Heavenly Bridal Chamber. The highest of the heavens.

REDEEMED REDEEMER--The Gnostic Christ, who has to be saved from death before he can save his brethren.

SHEKHINAH--A first century Jewish version of God's Presence (from sh-ch-n, "to dwell"), often synonymous with the Holy Spirit (Hebrew ruach, feminine gender). Her anthropomorphic characterization shows that she embodied traits of the ancient Mother Goddess. Indeed, Jewish mystics looked upon Shekhinah as God's feminine nature, from which human souls were descended, for which reason she was called "Matronit", or "Queen".

SOPHIA--Greek for "Wisdom". In books such as Proverbs, Sirach, Job, etc., God's creative "Wisdom" has anthropomorphic attributes, suggesting that "Sophia" was once a prehistoric deity. In NT books, "Wisdom" is the pre-existent Son of God; in certain Jewish and Gnostic works, "Wisdom" is female, either the "wife" of Cod, or the "daughter" of God. In Gnostic texts, the former becomes the Greater Sophia, or Heavenly Mother, the latter the Lesser Sophia, or the Son's spouse, Often there are several generations of "Sophias", descending in rank from the Heavenly Mother to the earthly wife of Jesus, Sometimes Sophia is even allegorized as Christ's spiritual wife, the Church.

SOWD--OT Hebrew for "assembly", "circle of people in council", "confidential talk, secrets", therefore, the precursor of NT Greek musterion, "mystery". KJV translates SOWD as "secret" (e.g. Amos 3:7, where it literally means "what is going on in the Heavenly Council"), Basically, SOWD refers to the Council in Heaven, but by extension, all heavenly secrets.

STATUS QUO ANTE--The pristine state at the beginning. Gnostic eschatology (q.v.) held that salvation would consist of a return to the original condition of things ("Paradise regained").

SYZYGY--A male-female pair of gods.

TETRAD--The extension of the Triad (q.v.) into a family of four (Father-Mother-Son-Son's wife), by marrying the Son to a wife (usually his "sister"). Thus, the Son "does what the Father does", Ritual "Sacred Marriages" (see hieros gamos), generally celebrated the Son's wedding, rather than the Father's.

TETRAGRAMMATON--The unspeakable name of God, YHWH, also thought by medieval Jews to secretly represent the Tetrad (q.v.), suggesting that God is really a family.

THERAPEUTAE--A pre-Christian ascetic sect dwelling in Lower Egypt, described by Philo. They were probably a radical Jewish offshoot, similar to the Essenes. They appear to have contributed to the later Christian idea of monasticism.

TRAJECTORY--Robinson's and Koester's term for a historical process, esp. the dynamic career of an idea, or complex of, ideas. Chosen to suggest that theology and dogma are often fluid rather than static, hence describe a "path or "direction" of development, "Trajectories" are to be distinguished from Gospel Message (kerygma), which was fixed at the moment of its revelation.

TRIAD--The Divine Family at the head of early Semitic pantheons, i.e. Father-Mother-Son. The lesser gods were also bene ha-elohim, "sons of God", brothers of the chief Son.

UNKNOWN FATHER--The highest Gnostic God, higher than Yahweh, correspond-ing to El in the ancient Triad.

VALENTINIANS--An early Gnostic sect, which gave us the Gospel of Philip. They appear to have been a moderate group, still close to Primitive Christianity, though their successors developed bizarre extremes of doctrine which deviated more and more from the Church's original beliefs.

YAHWISM--The monotheistic doctrine that there is only one God, Yahweh (Jehovah), It proscribed Israel's former polytheism and reference to divine sexuality in view of the immoral excesses to which the old religion had sunk (Ex. 32).

-ABBREVIATIONS-

From the Dead Sea Scrolls:

   1QS--The Community Rule (Serek Scroll).

   1QH--The Hymn Scroll

   1QM--The War Between the Sons of Light and the Sons of Darkness,

   CD---The Damascus Covenant

   See also Bibliography, p. 59.

Various sects of "orthodox" Christianity are apparently beginning to show their deep concern over the "mileage" that Latter Day Saints have been getting out of the newly discovered manuscripts from the intertestamental and early Christian eras, particularly those known as the "Dead Sea Scrolls" and the "Nag Hammadi texts".

The reasons for this are rather obvious. Mormonism claims to be a restoration of doctrines formerly taught by the Primitive Church and by inspired prophets since the beginning of time, Now, quite unexpectedly, these very doctrines--revealed by Joseph Smith to a shocked and startled world a hundred and fifty years ago--have begun to reappear in the writings of early Jews and Christians. The world is suddenly obliged to explain just how an uneducated farm-youth in frontier America was able to even name such beliefs as "three levels in heaven", human pre-existence, a Heavenly Mother, eternal marriage, the bearing of posterity after the Resurrection, man's divine origin and destiny, and many others, doctrines which no Christian sect of the time had ever heard of, let alone discussed or accepted.

Thoughtful persons everywhere have been impressed by this extraordinary phenomenon, Though the real strength of Mormonism lies in its dynamic vision of Man and his relationship to God, the fact that its teachings so closely parallel these newly recovered beliefs has convinced many that Joseph Smith's revelations were not drawn from imagination, but correspond to actual, historic realities. Since Mormonism is now the fastest growing religion in many parts of the world, the ministers of "orthodox" congregations are beginning to react with alarm. A veritable avalanche of anti-Mormon literature is presently being circulated with the hope of stemming the growth of the Latter Day Saints. And it is scarcely to be wondered at that one of the chief areas of concern is the support which these recent manuscript discoveries provide for the unique claims of Mormonism.

Melaine Layton has therefore entered the fray with a hastily prepared booklet entitled <u>The Truth About the Dead Sea Scrolls and Nag Hammadi Writings in Reference to Mormonism</u> Wheeling, Ill, 1979). Although her pamphlet contains some interesting information about Gnosticism and related topics, it turns out to be virtually worthless as a comparison of Mormon claims and the early documents, for it is based on two fundamental misunderstandings, which completely invalidate the hoped-for results.

The first "misunderstanding" is summed up neatly in Norman Geisler's Fore-ward, which hopefully opines that "it is ill-advised for Mormons to insist that these early Jewish and Christian cults are *early forms of Mormonism*" (italics added). As will be presently seen, no responsible Mormons have ever made such a claim. Thus, Ms. Layton's laborious efforts to inform us what the Essenes and Gnostics "really believed" are an exercise in futility.

The second "misunderstanding" is that Einar Erickson's lectures on the Qumran and Nag Hammadi texts are representative of serious Mormon scholarship, and that a refutation of them will be a refutation of Mormonism. This technique of "straw-man" will simply not do here, for Ms. Layton's criticisms are at best a criticism of Einar Erickson, not of the Mormon position. This any intelligent reader should be able to perceive for himself.

(In all fairness, it should be pointed out that Brother Erickson admits to being merely a "popularizer", and as such has made no attempt to organize the new material into patterns which might satisfy the scholar and his search for historical connections. While this alone can reveal the ultimate significance of these texts, Bro. Erickson has done an outstanding job of communicating the excitement and importance of the new finds to uncritical audiences. At the very worst, he has made no greater errors in detail than Ms. Layton, and most of his work remains perfectly sound, though Ms. Layton has omitted to inform her readers of this.)

What, then, is the real significance of this new material for the study of Mormonism and Christian origins?

First of all, it shows with staggering clarity that what now passes for "orthodoxy" was at the beginning only one of many initial responses to Christ's Gospel message.

Even the Bible is filled with an amazing plurality of theological opinions and doctrines, a fact which can easily be gathered from works such as Gerhard Hasel's two excellent summaries, Old Testament Theology: Basic Issues in the Current Debate (Grand Rapids, 1972), and New Testament Theology: Basic Issues in the Current Debate (Grand Rapids, 1978).

One should also contemplate the vast number of Jewish and Christian sects which have been spawned over the centuries by the same "infallible" Word of God to realize that no clear-cut agreement ever existed in Scripture concerning many issues of faith and dogma.

Christ's message (which presumably was devoid of contradiction when he himself first uttered it) appears to have been immediately "subject to a plurality of understandings" on the part of his listeners (James M, Robinson and Helmut Koester, Trajectories Through Early Christianity, Philadelphia, 1971. 26). From a single Gospel message there quickly developed such diverse schools of thought as the Apologetes and the Alexandrians, the Pauline theology leading from Ephesians to 1 Peter, Luke, Acts and the Pastorals, and a companion stream leading from Colossians and parts of the other Epistles to what was eventually termed "heresy"- Ibid., 10). As a matter of fact, the writings of Paul and John became the favorite source of "Gnostic" speculation for years to come, being employed as the very fountain-head of Gnostic anthropology, Christology and sacramental theology (Elaine Pagels, The Gnostic Paul, Philadelphia, 1975, 10; The Johannine Gospel in Gnostic Exegesis, Nashville, 1973).

But the non-canonical literature shows even more clearly that a pluralism of thought existed from the very beginning. The fact that much of it was used extensively by the Primitive Church shows that we cannot reject it out of hand as authentic doctrine.

1 Enoch, for example, was one of the books most prized by the early Christians; it was drawn upon no less than 128 times in the New Testament itself (R. H. Charles, Book of Enoch, London, 1913, xcv-xcix). The Savior also saw fit to quote from the Testaments of the Twelve Patriarchs (Joseph 28:2 = Matt. 5:44; Levi 13:5 = Matt, 6:19), showing that he too valued this early source.

The Shepherd of Hermas was perhaps the most widely read book in the entire Church from the 2nd until the 4th centuries (The Ante-Nicene Fathers, ed. Roberts and Donaldson, II:6). One must also not forget such widely valued Christian texts as 2 Baruch, 4 Ezra and the Odes of Solomon, if we are to get an accurate picture of what the early Church considered to be legitimate "Christian" Scripture. In fact, some of these apocryphal books which survive today "no doubt represent the books which were most highly prized among the Christians" (D. S. Russell, The Method and Message of Jewish Apocalyptic, Philadelphia, 1964, 34).

Thus, "for historical inquiry, the New Testament itself has no special claim to have made the correct and orthodox use of the criterion of true faith...New sources from recent discoveries...must be considered as historically of equal value with the canonical writings, they cannot be depreciated by reason of their non-canonical nature" (Koester, in Trajectories, 118-9).

"Walter Bauer, well-known as a lexicographer, but unfortunately little known as a historian of the ancient Church, demonstrated convincingly in a brilliant monograph of 1934 (Rechtglaubigkeit und Ketzerei im altesten Christentum) that Christian groups later labeled heretical actually predominated in the first two or three centuries, both geographically and theologically. Recent discoveries, especially those at Nag Hammadi in Upper Egypt, have made it even clearer that Bauer was essentially right, and that a thorough and extensive reevaluation of early Christian history is called for" (ibid., 114).

Secondly, the new disclosures enable us for the first time to organize what was once terra incognita into meaningful, historical patterns. It is this dynamic picture that we are looking for, with its successive phases interconnected in such a way as to reveal the vital movements that intersect with the Christian Community at the time of the Savior.

Thus, the Dead Sea Scrolls show with vastly improved clarity what immediately preceded Christianity; and the Nag Hammadi texts reveal for the first time important tendencies which emerged immediately thereafter. Most important of all, one can begin to see how at the "meridian of time" the beliefs of the Lord's own circle coincided with certain of these dynamic movements. Hence, as never before, Christian origins and doctrines are placed in a historical context which recognizes new "trajectories" (to borrow Koester's term) leading from Jewish apocalyptic to Primitive Christianity, and thence to what was eventually condemned as "heresy".

Recent advances in our understanding of the Gospel of John illustrate the results of this historical reorientation. Thanks to the new discoveries, John no longer dangles tentatively in the 2nd or 3rd centuries, where suspected "outside" influences used to place it. The revelations of the Dead Sea Scrolls show instead that the Fourth Gospel fits perfectly in the 1st century milieu of Palestine and Primitive Christianity.

At the same time, the ancient "heresy" called Gnosticism is now recognized to be no "outside" influence acting on John, but the outcome of legitimate tendencies within John and Christianity, tendencies which in turn were derived at least in part from the apocalyptic Judaism that included the Essenism of the Dead Sea Scrolls.

Thus, a newly recognized "trajectory" which culminated in Gnosticism becomes an important witness for the Judeo-Christian milieu out of which it grew. When properly understood, it shows that the documents from the Dead Sea indeed bear a profound relationship to the Nag Hammadi writings and Christianity, contrary to what Ms. Layton says on page 3 of her pamphlet. But even more, it shows that these documents have a profound relationship to Mormonism, which claims to coincide with the beliefs of the Primitive Church.

It is very important, then, that we analyze in some detail the history of this significant "trajectory", which has been called "gnosticizing", because it contains the seeds of fully-grown Gnosticism.

Let us start at the culmination and work backwards.

If we take "Gnosticism" to mean that system which includes a "Redeemed Redeemer" and an inferior Demiurge who created the material world, we must look entirely within Christianity for its origins, Edwin Yamauchi's exhaustive summary of proposed theories concerning Gnostic beginnings (Pre-Christian Gnosticism, Grand Rapids, 1973) excludes the possibility of such a Gnosticism prior to Christianity, inasmuch as the evidence now proves that the "Redeemed Redeemer" was strictly "a post-Christian development dependent upon the figure of Christ" *(op,* cit., 165), Earlier theories deriving him from the Iranian Gayomart have been abandoned, since alleged features connecting him with the "Redeemed Redeemer" considerably post-date Christianity, and cannot be demonstrated in pre-Christian Iranian thought.

The inferior Demiurge, once thought to derive from Platonism, likewise turns out to be purely Christian, being largely polemic against the Creator-God of the Jews (though it must have developed independently of the canonical view that Christ himself was the Creator of the world).

If we slightly enlarge our definition of "Gnosticism" to include the hierarchy of "aeons" (those angelic beings who mediate between Light and Matter) the sources are still largely Christian, e.g. the Pauline "powers and principalities" who control the elements (Gal, *4:3, 9;* Eph. *6:12:* Col. 1:16; etc.). In this case however, we begin to recognize sources still older than the Church, namely the angelology of Jewish apocalyptic, and the OT "sons of God" who rule over the nations (LXX Deut, 32: 8-9).

Yet, if we employ the broadest possible definition of "Gnosticism", i.e. the belief in a transcendent world which is man's true home, we find that the sources are equally at home in Christianity, heterodox Judaism, Mandaeism, Manichaeism, Zoroastrianism and the Hellenistic Mystery religions. It was the very ubiquity of this belief that misled early scholars, who--recognizing its widespread presence outside of Christianity--wondered if the entire Gnostic phenomenon did not have a pre-Christian, or non-Christian, origin.

We must therefore recognize several layers of Gnostic thought. At the bottom is a general "pre-Gnostic" foundation, considerably antedating Christianity. It is presently customary to refer to this broad base as "Gnosis", "proto-Gnosticism", or simply "gnosticism" (uncapitalized).

Above it lie the more specialized forms of "incipient" or genuine Gnosticism, which are already Christian in their basic belief. By general consent, reached at Messina in 1966, the name "Gnosticism" (capitalized) should be reserved for these specifically Christian phenomena (Ugo Bianchi, ed., Le Origini dello Gnosticismo, Leiden, 1967).

"Gnosticism" per se, then, is presently recognized to be a form of Christianity, interpreting the Christian message in terms of categories inherited from "Gnosis". It is most important; however, that we realize this was not simply the juxtaposition of separate traditions, for the earliest forms of both <u>coincided</u> in the theology of the Primitive Church. The first Christianity, in other words, already contained an indigenous form of belief which was itself "proto-Gnostic", and which later developed--along the "gnosticizing trajectory"--into fully developed Gnosticism, or Gnostic Christianity.

Common to the basic "Gnosis" was some form or other of dualism, i.e. the existence side by side of the <u>two</u> worlds: Light and Darkness, Good and Evil, Heaven and Earth, etc., Although specialists are wont to insist on technical differences between, say, the "eschatological" dualism of Qumran and the "cosmic" dualism of late Gnosticism,* it is *very* doubtful that the average believer was aware of such philosophical niceties. For him there were simply two worlds, the present "kingdom of earth", ruled over by Evil, and subject to corruption and death, and the "kingdom of heaven", already waiting with God, and in which spiritual values and immortality will prevail. The so-called "ethical" dualism found in both the Dead Sea Scrolls and the <u>Gospel</u> <u>of</u> <u>John</u> is but a moral reflection of this more basic dualism, and it would be short-sight to deny any connection between it and the "cosmic" dualism of later Gnosticism.

The mysterious statement of Jesus concerning the two worlds is generally characteristic of Gnosis: "My kingdom is not of this world" John 18:36). Indeed, it originated "out of the world...before the world was" (170:-63. This transcendent origin includes the disciples too, for they "are not of the world, even as I am not of the world" (vs. 16), having been "chosen...in him <u>before</u> the foundation of the world" (Eph. 1:4).

This idea that certain things had a <u>prior</u> existence <u>out</u> <u>of</u> <u>the</u> <u>world</u> "has a long history in the Biblical and early Jewish tradition" R:G. Hamerton-Kelly, <u>Pre-Existence,</u> <u>Wisdom</u> <u>and</u> <u>the</u> <u>Son</u> <u>of</u> <u>Man</u>, Cambridge, 1973, 15). The prophets themselves taught that the heavenly world contained the pre-existent things, which chosen seers were able to visit and observe (<u>ibid.</u>, 16). Even <u>Exodus</u> describes a Heavenly Temple, whose pattern Moses was to copy for the Tabernacle in the wilderness (25:9; of. 2 <u>Baruch</u> 4:2-7).

The older Semites likewise believed that the original models of earthly things pre-existed in heaven (Albright, <u>From</u> <u>the</u> <u>Stone</u> <u>Age</u> <u>to</u> <u>Christianity</u> (FSAC), N.Y., 1957, 177; Mircea Eliade, <u>The</u> <u>Myth</u> <u>of</u> <u>the</u> <u>Eternal</u> <u>Return,</u> Princeton, 19, 7-8). The pre-existence of man is strongly suggested in Babylonian tablets which describe the creation of the first couple out of the <u>blood</u> of slain gods, for the soul <u>(nephesh)</u> is in the blood (Gen. 9:4). Their names therefore have the cuneiform sign for "deity" placed before them, suggesting their divine origin (Seidel, <u>The</u> <u>Babylonian</u> <u>Genesis,</u> Chicago, 1937, 67-8).

----

*"Eschatological" dualism is the division between what presently appears on earth and what is destined to appear when God's kingdom is established. "Cosmic" dualism entails a further refinement of the distinction between God's kingdom and earth, namely, that of "spirit" and "matter".

This origin of the soul in the heavens was taught through several millennia of Semitic astral theology (Franz Cumont, Astrology and Religion Among the Greeks and Romans, reprint, N.Y., 1960, 6, 21-2, 40-1; Oriental Religion in Roman Paganism, reprint, N.Y., 1956, 125-6), which held that the substance of the soul was derived from the same divine "fire" as the gods. Even Philo (20 B.C. - 40 A.D.), who claimed that everything he taught agreed with the Pentateuch, believed that the soul pre-existed in the heavens before entering the body (De Somniis 1:22: De Cherubim 120), The OT accordingly contains obvious traces of belief in a divine, pre-existent Adam (Job 15:7), as well as the pre-existence of other men (Jer. 1:5).

The Essenes, whom most scholars identify with the sectaries of Qumran, also held this doctrine of the soul's pre-existence.

"Indeed, it is a firm belief among them that although bodies are corruptible, and their matter unstable, souls are immortal and endure forever; that, come from subtlest ether, they are entwined with bodies which serve them as prisons, drawn down as they are by some physical spell" (Josephus, Wars II.8:154).

Every member of the Community was "chosen by God from all eternity to become one of the elect. In preference to thousands of his fellow Jews, he had been loved by God from before Creation" (Geza Vermes, The Dead Sea Scrolls in English, Harmondsworth, 1968, 35). The Essenes therefore "called themselves God's eternal planting, for they believed that their Community would survive the period of the world's destruction, since it had originated in the heavenly world" (Lucetta Mowry, The Dead Sea Scrolls and the Early Church, Notre Dame, 1966, 45),

The concept that an entire community pre-existed together has recently been judged a "commonplace of apocalyptic thought" (Norman Perrin, Rediscovering the Teaching of Jesus, N.Y., 1967, 171: Hamerton-Kelly, op. cit., 9, 39, 105, 128, 152. 222). One can read of it, for instance, in 1 Enoch, which describes the pre-existent Community of the Elect before its sowing on earth:

> From the beginning the son of Man was hidden, and the Most High preserved him in the Presence of His might, and revealed him to the elect; and the Congregation of the elect shall be sown (cf. Matt. 13:38!, and the elect shall stand before him on that day (62:7-8).

The resulting idea of corporate pre-existence "was often expressed by means of the term 'mystery' (musterion), which referred to the hidden pre-existent things" (Hamerton-Kelly, p. cit., 9-10). This is particularly interesting because it has recently been shown that the NT word "mystery" was derived from the Hebrew SOWD, which referred to the pre-existent "Council in heaven", the same glimpsed in vision by Isaiah, Jeremiah and Ezekiel (H. Wheeler Robinson, "The. Council of Yahweh", Journal of Biblical Studies, 1944, 151-7).

This "heavenly Council" was an early form of the pre-existent Community, of which the sectaries at Qumran claimed to be a living part (4 Q Serek Shirah, the "Angelic Liturgy"), The pre-existent Community of apocalyptic became the pre-existent Church of

Primitive Christianity (Albert Schweizer, The Mysticism of the Apostle Paul, reprint N.Y., 1968, 102ff; 116; Jean Danielou, The Theology of Jewish Christianity (TJC)*, London, 1964, 4, 262-301), and, eventually, the "Pleroma", or the "All", of the Gnostics.

This pre-existent Community can further be seen in such works as the Qumran Hymn Scroll:

> All these things thou didst establish in Thy wisdom. Thou didst appoint all thy works before ever creating theme the host of Thy spirits and the Congregation of Thy Holy Ones, the heavens and all their hosts...for Thou hast established them from before eternity (1QH 13:7-10).

1QH 8:4-11 refers to this Community as "a Mystery...a tree fed from a secret spring ,,.whose stock lies beneath a perpetual font", We read of it again in various rabbinic commentaries as the "pre-existent Israel" (Jewish Encyclopedia, N.Y., 1905,. X:183). In Christian apocalyptic it became an "invisible City" or "heavenly Zion" (4Ezra 7:26; 9:38--10:51), or the "Old Woman" "for whom all things were later created (2 Clement 14:1; Shepherd of Hermas V. 2, 4:1), This pre-existent Church also appears in the NT as the "heavenly Jerusalem, the Mother of us all" (Gal, 4:26; Rev. 21:2). "This new city of freedom already exists in heaven where Christ is,.. But it also exists on earth in the Church, the body of Christ, whose members are *colonists from heaven* sent to prepare men for the full establishment of God's kingdom and Christ's second coming" (italics added; Raymond T, Stamm, in Interpreter's Bible X:541).

But the pre-existence of individual souls is even more widely attested in early Jewish and Christian literature. We have already referred to the Essene and Philonic doctrines of pre-existent souls. The Wisdom of Solomon speaks of these individual souls as follows: "As a child I was by nature well endowed, and a good soul fell to my lot; or rather, being good, I entered an undefiled body" (8:19-20). Apocalyptists generally taught that these souls dwelled in a special chamber (or chambers), awaiting their turn to descend into bodies (4 Ezra 4:37-43; 2 Baruch 23:3-5; 2 Enoch 23:4-5s 49:2; a fragment of this can still be found in Rev. 9: 11!) .

The rabbis for a time held the same belief. In the Talmud and Misrash, for example, the special chamber is called the guf (Abodah Zarah 5a; Yebamoth 62:1; Sifre 143b), or araboth (Chagiga 12b), According to the Genesis Rabbah, God took counsel with the pre-existent souls before creating the earth (8). The Tanhuma Pekude actually records a conversation in which God explains to one of these souls how it is to descend into matter, and that if it will obey the Torah righteously, it will one day return to his presence to enjoy everlasting bliss (3), (See also F, Weber, Jüdische Theologie, Leipzig, 1897, 212, 225ff., for a treatment of Jewish pre-existence doctrine.)

----

*Danielou defines "Jewish Christianity" as the earliest Christian belief, still expressed in the thought forms of Judaism, prior to Gentile influence, not to be confused with H. J. Schoeps' Ebionism, or those who upheld the Jewish Law (Acts 15).

The Church Fathers continued to teach human pre-existence for several centuries, as attested in the works of Origen, Justin Martyr, Cyril of Jerusalem, Pierius, John of Jerusalem, Rufinus, Nemesius, and many others (Hastings, Encyclopedia of Religion and Ethics X:239). "Orthodox" Christianity is therefore beginning to grudgingly admit that pre-existence was an important part of the Church's original teaching. (Interpreter's Dictionary of the Bible, Nashville, 1962, III:869-70; Hastings Dictionary of the Bible, N.Y., 1963, ad loc; Adolph von Harnack, History of Dogma, reprint, N,Y. 1961, I:318-331; Johannes Beumer, "Die altchristliche Idee einer praexistierenden Kirche", Wissenschaft und Weisheit 9, 13-22; H. Schlier, Der Brief an die Epheser, Dusseldorf, 1957, 49-50; etc..

Recent scholars have begun to discover a growing number of passages in the NT which are dependent upon the doctrine of pre-existence. The disciples' question concerning the blind man ("Master, who did sin, this man, or his parents, that he was born blind?" John 9:2) shows that they recognized the possibility of having sinned in a pre-existent life (Interpreter's Dictionary of the Bible III:869).

Hamerton-Kelly has exhaustively examined many other NT passages which presuppose the doctrine of pre-existence. These include Matt, 13:33ff; 25:34; Rom. 8:28-30; 1 Cor. 3:5-17; 5:1-10; Col, 1:5, 18, 26ff; 2:2-3; Eph. 1:22-23; 2:19-22; 4:16; 1 Tim. 6:1:19; 2 Tim. 4:8, 18; Heb. 2:11; 12:22-23; Jude 6; Rev. 3:12; 12:1ff, in addition to several others we have already mentioned (John 17:6, 16; Gal, 4:26; Eph. 1:4; Rev. 21:2; op. cit., ad loc.).

The next generation of Christian texts deals even more explicitly with human pre-existence, beginning with the Odes of Solomon, dated somewhere near the end of the 1st century. In the opinion of J.H Charlesworth, the Odes served as "a tributary to Gnosticism which flows from Jewish apocalyptical mysticism", as well as a 1st century Christian "hymn book" ("The Odes of Solomon", Catholic Biblical Quarterly 31, 369). According to these "Christian hymns", the soul "originated in the heights" (Ode 22); "From another race am I, for the Father of Truth remembered me. He possessed me from the beginning, for His bounty begot me" (Ode 41). One is especially reminded of the Qumran texts when the Odist compares the eschatological Community to "fruit-bearing trees" whose crown is "self-grown", and whose roots are "from an immortal land", watered by a "river of gladness" (Ode 11, Charlesworth ed.).

The earliest Nag Hammadi texts were written slightly later than the Odes. For a while, they remained "incomparably closer to normative Christianity" than any previously known Gnostic works (K. Grobel, The Gospel of Truth, Nashville, 1960, 15). In fact, the older ones remain "fairly close to the 'orthodox' Church down to about 180" (R. McLain Wilson, The Gospel of Philip, London, 1962, 4). This shows how intimately "Gnostic" ideas were originally rooted in Christianity, and how they gradually developed out of it, especially the critical idea of human pre-existence.

Thus, the Gospel of Philip (ca. 140 A.D.) quotes Jesus as saying, "Blessed is he who is before he came into being. For he who is both was and shall be. The highness of man is not revealed, but is in secret" (Sayings 57-8). This is very likely an authentic saying of the Savior, for it is also found in the Gospel of Thomas ("Blessed is he who was

16

before he came into being"; Logion 17), being apparently based on "a sayings collection...more primitive than the canonical gospels" (Robinson and Koester, op. cit ,, 186).

According to Thomas, it is the secret knowledge of one's true nature which assures immortality. "Jesus said, Have you then discovered the beginning, so that you inquire about the end? For where the beginning is, there shall be the end. Blessed is he who shall stand at the beginning, and he shall know the end, and he shall not taste death" (Logion 18).

This mysterious beginning is further explained in another saying: "Jesus said, If they say to you, From where have you originated? Say to them, We have come from the Light, where the Light has originated through itself. If they say to you, Who are you? Say, We are His sons and we are the elect of the Living Father" (Logion 50).

The Gospel of Truth also affirms man's divine origin. "They know that they had come forth out of him like children from an adult man" (27:11-14; of. Acts 17:28; Heb. 12:9). As in Thomas, the end of these pre-existent souls is return to the source: "Him from whom the beginning went forth, Him to whom all shall return who came out of Him and became manifest to the glory and joy of His name" (38:1-6). This, again, is the ultimate secret of immortality: "For he who has no root also has no fruit, but thinking to himself, I have come to be...He shall perish of himself. Therefore he who was not at all also will not become" (28:16-24).

Since the true home of these pre-existent souls is not earth, but heaven, the believers are counseled to "become passersby", relinquishing all claim on mortality (Gospel of Thomas, Log. 42). In this way, they should follow Jesus, who "had not where to lay his head" (Log, 86 = Matt. 8:201 Lk. 9:26). "Passersby" do not search for earthly manna, as did their Jewish fathers (John 6:58), but for the "bread of life", prepared in heaven (vs. 50ff), or the "Truth"--that peculiar Johannine word which designates "divine reality" (aletheia), in contrast to the world.

The true disciples, therefore, are "strangers" and "pilgrims" passing through an earthly city in search of their heavenly home (Heb. 11:13-16). Philo already expressed this "theology of the pilgrim" (Koester, in Trajectories, 140-1) when he wrote that we are only "wanderers" through the world "as in a foreign city, in which before birth we had no part, and in this city does but sojourn until he has exhausted his appointed span of life" (De Cherubim 120). One group of Gnostics even called itself "Peratics" (Gr, perao, "to pass through" to express the belief that men are aliens from a heavenly race, exiled in the material world. Like their master, the Homeless Wisdom (cf, John 1:5, 11-14), they are homeless "strangers" wandering through the lone and dreary "wilderness", whose faith alone assures them of attaining their spiritual goal (Heb. 11:1ff).

As Friedrich Schiele demonstrated some time ago, this is probably the real meaning of the word "Hebrew", to whom the NT epistle was addressed. According to him, the "Hebrews" would have been participants in a spiritualizing Temple-cult, reliving symbolically their journey through the world in search of a heavenly, home ("Harnack's 'Probabilia' Concerning the Address and the Author of the Epistle to the Hebrews", American Journal of Theology 9, 1910, 290-308). Unlike the Israelites, however, these

17

new "Hebrews" would be able to penetrate through the veil of the Temple, and gain direct access to the Presence of God (Heb. 10:19-20).

Now that the Nag Hammadi texts have supplied so many of the missing links in this pre-existence "trajectory", we recognize that the so-called "Gnostic" pre-existence doctrine is really evidence for the continuation of the Church's own doctrine, from which it was derived! This is all the more certain because we now know what the pre-Christian sources taught, as well, and can trace a continuous "trajectory" describing Man's origin in the celestial world which lasted for several hundred years. Thus, "Christian Gnosticism emerge(s) as a reaffirmation, though in somewhat different terms, of the original transcendence central to the very beginnings of Christianity" (James Robinson, The Nag Hammadi Library, N.Y., 1977, 4).

The "different terms" in this case refer to the Gnostic's growing contempt for the body, and his conviction that the "Resurrection" was merely a demonstration of the spirit's superiority over matter (see below).

An intermediate stage appears in the 2nd century Epistle to Rhinos, which (though it insists the resurrection of the body is no illusion; 48:6-16) interprets the phenomenon as the clothing of the soul in "spiritual flesh", after the fashion of 1 Cor. 15:44.

Nevertheless, the ubiquitous pre-existence scenario--which is the least common denominator of all these historical developments--remains identical throughout. It consists of: a)--the soul's heavenly origin, b)--its "fallen" state on earth, and c)--its return whence it came, whether in or out of the body.

For a positive comparison with Mormon theology, this is the minimum that is required, though we would add that Mormonism, like the Primitive Church, teaches the literal resurrection of the body.

IV

Nevertheless, in spite of the growing body of evidence that the Primitive Church taught the pre-existence of the soul, even a scholar like Hamerton-Kelly occasionally betrays his traditional reluctance to admit pre-existence back into the theology of "orthodox" Christianity.

Speaking of God's "foreknowledge" in Rom. 8:28-30, he cautiously writes that "the Christians were chosen by God for salvation sometime before they began to experience it. 'When did this election take place?' one may ask...Most commentators believe that it took place in the eternal counsels of God, before the creation of the world...There is some reason, however, to believe that something more 'concrete' than foreordination is in mind here...Such a meaning would entail that the believer existed in some form more substantial than an idea...The verb ("foreknow") therefore faintly implies that the elect (8:33) really existed when the choice was made" (italics added; op, cit., 154-5).

But reluctant or not, Hamerton-Kelly dutifully concludes after painstaking analysis that Primitive Christianity did teach a real kind of human pre-existence, equivalent to that of the pre-existent Christ. His conclusion, after studying Paul's epistle to the Corinthians, is that "Paul believed in two pre-existent entities, Christ and the Church" (italics added; op cit., 152). These "eschatologically pre-existent entities were identical with items that were believed, in the tradition from which they came, to have existed before the world" (ibid.). Man, in other words, had just as real a pre-existence as Christ, whose ante-mortal career even "orthodoxy" has never attempted to reduce to a mere "thought" in God's mind;

Hamerton-Kelly's inclusion of the word "faintly" in the previous quotation, however, still betrays the scholar's extreme caution when introducing an idea which he anticipates will be resisted by the rank-and-file of "orthodox" believers;

The Dutch Jesuit, Johannes Beumer, was even more nervous when admitting the inescapable fact that pre-existence was widely taught by Primitive Christianity.

"Now, there is in the early Christian literature an idea which is easily over-looked", he writes, "which has found little attention in modern theological discussion...I mean the idea of a pre-existent Church" (op. cit., 14).

Yet, after producing several pages of irrefutable evidence in support of this early belief, he anxiously recognizes what a problem its acceptance would create for modern "orthodoxy".

"If the idea of a pre-existent Church is therefore true, and cannot be denied, we must ask just what does this concept really mean?" (italics added; ibid., 17).

In growing desperation, he insists that "it is most important we determine whether or not we have a theologically sound explanation according to the body of faith!" (italics added, ibid., 17).

After disallowing the possibility that the Church originally understood human pre-existence in the literal sense, he gratuitously suggests that we take it to mean merely existence in God's "thought"--which is no pre-existence at all!

And why? Because "we must consider the idea of a real pre-existence *irreconcilable* with the *basic concepts of Christianity*" (italics added; ibid., 20, meaning, of course, modern, "orthodox" Christianity!

It was von Harnack who (perhaps unwittingly) gave currency to the notion that pre-existence might be reduced to nothing more than "foreknowledge" in God's mind.

Actually, he recognized two kinds of "pre-existence".

"As the whole history of the world and the destiny of each individual are recorded in (God's) tablets or books, so also each thing is ever present before him" (italics added; op. cit. I:318).

In other words, there is that which "pre-exists" as God's knowledge, and that which pre-exists in actual fact. (See also Hamerton-Kelly, op. cit. 1-2). The former includes God's plan for history, the latter "everything of real value that from time to time appears on earth (and) has its existence in heaven" (italics added; von Harnack, op. cit. I:318).

Anxious traditionalists have chosen deliberately to recognize only von Harnack's first category of "thought pre-existence" (compare, for example, A, Ritschl's expression, "ideal pre-existence"), since it provides them with a convenient means of "demythologizing" what is incompatible with "orthodox" belief. It is now time that they reconsider his other category, which insists that a genuinely pre-existent thing "exists before-hand with God in the same way as it appears on earth, that is with all the *material attributes* belonging to its essence" italics added: ibid.).

This real pre-existence, he added, was the kind accepted by the "ancient Jews" and "the whole of the Semitic nations" (ibid.). As such, it cannot be attributed to Hellenic influences (ibid., I:103), but was an authentic inheritance from the Semitic past (see above), Further evidence of this is the fact that Hellenic pre-existence usually involved the idea of reincarnation, which was always foreign to Semitic thought.

Unfortunately, Judeo-Christian doctrine finally fell under the influence of gentile Hellenism, and it began to increasingly resemble Platonism, as some of the Gnostic evidence shows. But in no original sources do we ever find that the body (though presently "fallen") was truly despised,* Both Jews and Christians viewed the body as a "blessed vessel" (Epistle of Barnabas 21:7-8) in which to gain necessary experience. Indeed, the rabbis even held that the world in which one is tried and tested "is better than the one in which thou hast lived hitherto, and when I created thee it was only for this purpose" (Tanhuma Pekude 3). This necessity of physical experience is still alluded to in the 2nd century Gospel of Philip, which recalls that the fall of man, was actually prompted by the Holy Ghost! (Saying 16; compare also 1 Pet. 1:19-20, which shows that the necessity of an atonement was foreseen and foreordained before Creation,)

---

*However, it must be recalled that Jewish requirements for ritual purity prohibited bodily functions in the proximity of the Temple. As the Qumran Temple Scroll indicates, "the Temple and its city possessed the sanctity of the Sinaitic encampment and this required a three-day purification for admission" (Jacob Milgrom, "The Temple Scroll", Biblical Archaeologist 41:117), This desire to keep the Holy Community free of ritual pollution undoubtedly contributed to the ascetic attitude of later groups who fled to the desert to be closer to God.

To summarize, then, it is certain that the original pre-existence doctrine of Judaism and Christianity attributed a real heavenly existence to things before their appearance on earths "For before all things were visible, I used to go about in the invisible things, like the sun from east to west, and from west to east" (2 Enoch 24:4). It is especially important to note that these things were described as already created: "With the soul of Adam the souls of all the generations of man were created. They are stored up in a promptuary, in the seventh of the heavens, whence they are drawn as they are needed for human body after human body" (B. Chagiga 12b).

As such, they are every bit as real as the angels; "I (Jacob) am an angel of God, and a primeval spirit, the first born of all creation, and like me were Abraham and Isaac created before any other works of God" (Joseph's Prayer, in Origen, Commentary on John).

The Shepherd of Hermas also says unambiguously of the pre-existent Church: "She was created before all things...for her sake the world was framed" (V.2,4:1). In view of these and similar texts, it has rightfully been concluded that even God's "foreknowledge" of pre-existent things must be understood in the realistic sense that "foreknowledge" appears in Hos. 13:5: Amos 3:2 and Matt. 7123, where "to take note of", not "to foresee", is intended (Hamerton-Kelly, op. cit., 154).

V

Also of importance for a comparison of Mormonism and the ancient texts is the peculiar relationship of the Savior and mankind, which plays an important role in the Primitive Church's pre-existence "trajectory".

As indicated earlier, the main contribution made by the Church to the pre-existence scenario was the introduction of a "Redeemed Redeemer", or figure of Christ. Certain hints concerning a pre-existing, messianic figure already existed in the Jewish Wisdom literature and the Danielic Son of Man, showing that the idea of a coming Savior was not unknown to antiquity. But not until the actual advent of Jesus did such a figure emerge in full stature as the One chosen before Creation to redeem his "many brethren".

Traditional scholars long supposed that the peculiar association of Redeemed Redeemer and his literal brethren in Gnosticism was a phenomenon unique to "heresy". Thus, the source of a Gnostic Savior was erroneously sought for outside of Christianity. The present state of documentation, however, shows that no such "pre-" or "non-Christian" Redeemed Redeemer ever existed, and that his origins are essentially Christian, and cannot be understood apart from Christianity.

It is very significant, then, that the first Christian texts to describe the Redeemer and his mission already speak of the men whom he saves as his "many brethren" (Rom. 8:29; Heb. 2:11). This is the same relationship which the Gnostics insisted was to be understood realistically. This is particularly revealing because these two passages from the NT have already been connected by Hamerton-Kelly with the doctrine of human pre-existence! (see above). Since we know that the Primitive Church held both Christ and the Church to have pre-existed, both must have had the same heavenly origin. In short, both were literally "brethren" before Creation.

Ernst Kasemann has also detected this doctrine of suggeneia ("common origin") in Hebrews, which clearly states that "both he who sanctifies and they who are sanctified are of one origin (ex henos)" (2:11).

That this common origin lay not in some earthly ancestor, but in the Father himself, is inescapable.

"Jesus must be perfected, as well as his own", writes Kasemann. "In 2:10 many 'sons' are brought into conjunction with 'the Son', and he, as well as they, are ultimately descended (according to 2:11) 'from One', ex henos. It is totally irrelevant to think of this 'One' as Adam or Abraham, who are indeed not even under discussion. Since the purpose of vs. 11 is to establish a common bond between 'Son' and 'sons', this lineage can only be derived from God, who alone is the Father of Jesus" (Das wandernde Gottesvolk, Gottingen, 1961, 90).

This agrees with Paul's views in the Corinthian letters that there were two pre-existing entities, Christ and the Church. Since these were "espoused" from before Creation to comprise the Body of Christ (Eph. 1:4), they were necessarily consubstantial beings, as early glosses on Eph. 5:0 further indicate: "We are members of his body from his flesh and from his bones" (see Markus Barth, Anchor Bible, Ephesians, N.Y., 197k, 724), Thus, even the NT presupposes the common origin of men and Christ--a theme which was long supposed to reflect only "heretical" Gnostic influence.

But once again, the very scholars who are forced by the evidence to see the doctrine of suggeneia, or "consubstantiality", behind the doctrine of Christ and his "many brethren", are disturbed by the fact that "orthodox" Christianity can no longer accept such a belief.

After admitting that Christ and the Church pre-existed together in Paul's doctrine, Hamerton-Kelly, for example, backs down and suggests arbitrarily that Paul's conception "lacks the ingredient of consubstantiality between man and God" (op. cit., 153). And why is this? Because the Christian is not being restored to Adam's original state, but is "being transformed into the image of Christ" (ibid.).

Yet when pressed to explain what this "image of Christ" is, he confesses that it is the same pre-existent image "according to which Adam was created" (!) (ibid.).

In short, the same image which originally produced Adam is now "producing the new life of the redeemed". This is the doctrine of "how to reverse or escape from the disaster of creation and return to the status quo ante", and "would be essentially the same as the gnostic restitution to an original status" except that it has to wait for the eschaton, and because "it lacks the ingredient of consubstantiality" (italics added; ibid.).

Thus, Hamerton-Kelly argues in a circle, and merely restates his initial assumption, derived gratuitously from "orthodoxy". Fortunately, Markus Barth was not so queasy when affirming the doctrine of consubstantiality in the Ephesian glosses.

For all his skillful evasion, then, Hamerton-Kelly has still to conclude that man is returning to the same image of Christ and the Church that existed before Creation, and that it is the same image which is borne by the Body of Christ today.

Kasemann's case is even more interesting, Like Hamerton-Kelly, he feels obliged in the end to repudiate (in the name of "orthodoxy") what he laboriously proves with his voluminous evidence.

The bulk of Das wandernde Gottesvolk ("Gods Wandering People") aims at care-fully showing how Hebrews depends on the idea of Christ leading his literal brethren back along the path of salvation as archegos ("first of a series") and prodromos ("forerunner") (Heb. 2110; 6:20). This is, in fact, one of the outstanding works of scholarship supporting the L.D.S. view of pre-existence and man's essential relationship to Christ.

The presence of such a "Gnostic myth" in Hebrews, Kasemann states, "can be tested very concretely. The previous study has undoubtedly shown such strong parallels--both in basic motif and detail--between Hebrews and the myth that our attempt to postulate a common tradition behind both appears fully justified" (op. cit., 58).

This conclusion is stated even more strongly in the following passage.

"The Epistle to the Hebrews proves that the Primitive Christian Community did not hesitate to employ mythical formulations and ideas for its purposes. On the basis of the preceding study, we may say that the general conception of the Epistle, and its

Christology in particular, were made possible only by using an *already 'Gnostic' foundation"* (italics added; ibid., 110).

But then suddenly, for a couple of curiously detached pages, the scholar turns preacher, pausing to suggest that none of this was understood literally by the same Primitive Christians!

"For literalism (Naturalismus), with its concomitant Hellenistic world-view, is irreconcilable with the Christian revelation of Hebrews (!!). Consequently, any speculation about the pre-existence of souls or individuals--in other words, the entire structure of Gnostic mythology--becomes impossible" (emphasis added; ibid. 112).

Even so, he is forced to admit that verse 2:11--with its doctrine of suggeneia -- "keeps alive" this literal doctrine (ibid.), even making it part of the basic argument! Thus, again, the scholar finds himself arguing in a circle.

Why, then, did the author employ such "mythology" in the first place?

Because, Kasemann lamely answers, "this Gnostic motif gives Hebrews the opportunity to explain the relationship between Christ and his brethren" (!!) (ibid.).

In other words, without allowing the slightest possibility that such a "myth" could be actually believed, our ancient author chose to employ what he distinctly disagreed with, simply because it best illustrated what he was trying to say!

This must surely be one of the more subtle forms of scholarly logic.

Our present knowledge concerning the sequence of Christianity and Gnosticism, however, permits us to completely discount Kasemann's short lapse from otherwise masterful scholarship, for we now know that there was no Gnosticism prior to Hebrews --and certainly no Gnostic Redeemer--which could have influenced the writing of that early Epistle. The truth is that Primitive Christianity, with its themes of suggeneia and pre-existence, was what influenced Gnosticism! Meanwhile, Kasemann has shown once and for all that these themes support the whole argument of Hebrews., which can hardly be understood without them.

VI

The heavenly pre-existence and common ancestry (suggeneia) of Savior and Saved thus turn out to be Christianity's contribution to Gnosticism, rather than the other way around. Indeed, the roots of both concepts can already be detected in pre-Christian apocalyptic writings, such as I Enoch 62: 7-8 (see above), which describes the Son of Man and the Community of the Elect together in heaven prior to their being sown on earth. Next the NT affirms their common ancestry. Thus it only remained for the Gnostics to continue using both traditions as the basis for their myth of the Redeemed Redeemer, who leads his natural brethren back into the Light after being saved from death by the power of the Unknown Father.

This suggests how the newly discovered texts should be studied to determine whether certain ideas contained in them are merely "similar" to Mormon ideas, or have genuine, historical connections with early Christianity. Only those which can be organically linked to the Primitive Church are of value in supporting Mormon claims' neither arbitrary "parallelomania", nor Ms. Layton's inability to see the internal connections at all, is correct.

Furthermore, one must be careful to understand the actual claims of Mormonism. No informed Latter Day Saint would pretend that what appears in the Dead Sea Scrolls is "Mormonism", pure and simple. Indeed, the Book of Mormon long ago pointed out that what existed just prior to Christ was not Christianity, but the Law of Moses, which was observed exclusively until the Savior appeared (2 Nephi 25: 24-26). Paul also referred to what went before as the "Law", that "schoolmaster", whose function was to bring the Jews unto Christ (Gal. 3:24-25).

Neither could any Latter Day Saint claim that what appears in the Nag Hammadi texts is still "Mormonism", at least in its pure form. Long before the recent discoveries were made, Joseph Smith was told concerning such books that "many things contained therein are true", but that there were also "many things contained therein that are not true...Whoso readeth it, let him understand, for the Spirit manifesteth truth" (Doctrine and Covenants 91:1-4). Consequently, when he began to work on his "Inspired Version" of the Bible, he chose to omit all apocryphal works as generally "not needful" to Mormons (vs. 6).

Still, it would be foolish to conclude that the Dead Sea Scrolls contained no hints of Christianity to come, or the Nag Hammadi texts no recollections of the Christianity preceding. It is therefore desirable that we treat the entire literature--including the Bible--as connected "geologic strata", with the earliest material at the bottom, and the succeeding material arranged in layers above, though sometimes distorted, or interspersed with debris and foreign material. Like gold that has washed down the stream of history, the important doctrines must sometimes be disinterred from accompanying "overburden". But analysis reveals where the precious metal originated, and through which channels it moved before coming to rest. To deny the intervening connections would be like denying that oaks are related to acorns, though inevitable changes have made the similarities less obvious than the differences.

And yet, Brother Erickson's method of bypassing the historical analysis and going directly to the results reveals a surprising amount of true "gold"! This is not to be unexpected, since the Dead Sea Scrolls and the Nag Hammadi texts very obviously contain many of the doctrines Joseph Smith said were taught by early Jews and Christians, though strenuously denied by "orthodox" apologists. One would be foolish, then, not to pick up gold wherever it lies exposed, even if no scientific methods have been used to find it.

Even Ms. Layton's correspondents cannot avoid seeing some of this precious material.

"I concede that there are some striking similarities", writes one of them.

But he also appears to believe that these "striking similarities" will go any if he stresses their supposedly "non-orthodox" provenance, for he thereupon insinuatingly adds: "As you point out, such parallels do not confirm, they condemn if one considers the source of the parallels" (italics added; p. 54).

This is obviously a reference to the old argument that the sources are only "Gnostic", though as we have already seen, what we now label "Gnostic" was originally derived from legitimate Christianity. Ms. Layton unfortunately makes no attempt to understand this point.

Again, Ms. Layton never tires of pointing out that there are important dissimilarities between Mormonism and the ancient manuscripts (as if no Mormon scholar had ever noticed!), Yet, this is exactly what one would expect after Primitive Christianity entered into the world at large, interacting with Platonism, Neo-Platonism, Aristotelianism, oriental mystery-cults, Egyptian syncretism, heterodox Judaism, and the private exegeses of a thousand metaphysically-inclined theologians.

History actually records how Christianity rapidly evolved into Eastern orthodoxy, Western orthodoxy, Montanism, Arianism, Pelasgianism, Valentinianism, Nestorianism, Encratism, etc. etc. Yet no one denies that these had a common origin, in spite of their manifold differences. Why, then, disavow the Christian origins of Gnosticism, simply because it differs from so-called "orthodoxy"?

As a matter of fact, even "orthodoxy" is markedly split on important matters, such as Trinitarianism, the God of the Creeds, Creation out of nothing, the origin of the soul at birth, predestination, Mariolatry, the cult of Saints, infant baptism, sprinkling and immersion, transubstantiation, the merits of human virtue, the cult of Temple-worship, changes in ecclesiastical organization, works and faith, etc. etc. Biblical Christianity has everything today from self-ordained "evangelicals", who "take Jesus for their personal Savior", to sacramental priesthood, no priesthood at all, ascetics, those who marry, those who are saved by grace, those saved by the sacraments, "soul-sleepers", souls that go to Paradise, miracle healers, those who rely on doctors, those whose Sunday is the Lord's Day, those who observe the Jewish Sabbath, celibate priests, woman priests, preachers, determinists, advocates of free will, existentialists, fundamentalists, liberals, eucumenicals, Congregationalists, presbyters, etc., etc. Yet all of these different points of view claim to descend from the same Primitive Church, Why then pretend that certain dissimilarities between Mormonism and the ancient texts invalidate the important connections?

Ms. Layton has utterly failed to come to grips with this question. No matter what one thinks of the differences, the essential lines of filiation remain to be explained.

Nor is it any good facetiously suggesting far-fetched parallels between Mormonism and unrelated phenomena on the basis of trivial coincidences which can be found anywhere. We do not draw parallels unless we can also show factual organic connections between them, as is certainly the case with the Dead Sea Scrolls, Christianity and the Nag Hammadi texts. All of the important scholars today are doing the very same thing. Why else the great interest in the connections between these new finds and the Primitive Church?

VII

Let us now move on to other important parallels between Mormonism and the newly discovered texts from the time of the ancient Church.

The reader is by now aware that we affirm Mormonism to be a <u>restoration</u> of what was had in the Primitive Church. But there is an even broader claim associated with Mormonism, viz, that the Gospel of Christ is the <u>same</u> Eternal Gospel that had many times been revealed since the beginning of the human race. Only because of the recalcitrance of men did it disappear from time to time--being in fact replaced at the time of Moses by a lesser Law which Israel could understand and obey (Jos, Smith Version, <u>Exodus</u> 34:1-2; see below).

If God truly loves all mankind, there can be no doubt that he revealed himself to those who lived <u>before</u> Christ. This was actually the belief of the first Christians who claimed that the Gospel was preached to Abraham (<u>Gal</u>. 3:8), Moses (<u>1 Cor</u>. 10:4) and others, beginning with Adam and Eve (Eusebius, <u>History of the Church</u> 1. 3:4; Ambrose, <u>De Sacrum</u> 1:4; St. Augustine, <u>Epistolae Retrac.</u> 1.13:3; <u>Clementine Homilies; Revelation of Adam to His Son Seth; Apocryphon of John</u>; etc.). Even the Savior referred to earlier revelations of himself <u>Matt</u>, 19:8; <u>John</u> 5:39). Thus, it is no surprise that the Dead Sea Scrolls--and many other pre-Christian sources--contain various doctrines generally thought to be limited to Christianity.

The Qumran Community, for instance, had a surprising foreknowledge of the Johannine concept of the Holy Spirit as Paraclete ("advocate and witness of truth"; Raymond E. Brown, speech at Provo, Utah, 5/7/74).

Their Idea of the Congregation as a "temple" for the Lord's Spirit also fore-shadowed the Church's belief (<u>1QS</u> 5:5ff; 8:4ff; <u>1 Cor</u>. 3:11; <u>2 Cor</u>. 6:16; <u>Eph</u>. 2: 19-22; <u>2 Pet</u>, 2:5; see Bertil Gartner, <u>The Temple and the Community in Qumran,</u> Cambridge, 1965, 50, 60, etc.), This "spiritual Temple" occurs again in Mormonism, which calls its local units "stakes" in the "Tabernacle" of Zion (<u>Isa</u>. 33:20; 54:2; <u>Doct. and Cov</u>. 82:14; <u>Moses</u> 7:62), or the dwelling place of the "pure in heart"--an expression specifically associated with the Temple in ancient Judaism (Ps. 24:4; <u>Doct</u>. and <u>Cov</u>. 101,21-23). This human "Tabernacle"--like the Qumran and Christian "spiritual Temple"--was thought of as a Holy Community where the righteous could eventually "see God" (cf. <u>Matt</u>. 5:8). For this reason, both the Qumran "Saints" and the "Latter Day Saints" gathered "out of the world" to enjoy the blessings of God's unrestricted Presence (<u>Doct</u>. and <u>Cov</u>. 136,10-11, 31).

Both the Essenes and the Christians, however, insisted on the ultimate necessity of an <u>earthly</u> Temple which would serve as a ritual center for the Community, Even though the Qumran sectaries had temporarily rejected the Jerusalem Temple as "polluted", they looked forward to the restoration of a physical site in the New Jerusalem (<u>Temple Scroll)</u>. The Lord's disciples likewise "continued daily in the Temple" after the Ascension (<u>Lk</u>. 24:53; <u>Acts</u> 2:46; 3:1; etc.). Thus, the idea that the Community was itself a "Temple" in no way replaced the need for a physical cult-center. In fact, various Christians for several centuries continued to construct "Holies of Holies" for their "Bridal Chamber" rites (see below).

While it is true that Qumran temporarily claimed to be able to atone for Israel's sins without benefit of the sacrificial cult (1QS 9:4-5), this was no more unusual than Samuel's doctrine of obedience, "Hath the Lord as great delight in burnt offerings and sacrifices as in obeying the voice of the Lord? Behold, to obey is better than sacrifice, and to hearken than the fat of rams" (1 Sam. 15:22).

It is also certain that Jews before Christ referred to themselves as a "Church" (ekklesia), as stated in the Book of Mormon, especially when gathered together to hear the reading of the Law (Bauer-Arndt-Gingrich, A Greek-English Lexicon of the New Testament, Chicago, 1957, 240; of. esp. LXX Deut. 4:10; 9:10; etc.) According to Philo, the Hebrews became a Church when through faith they embarked on their cultic "exodus" out of Egypt (Quaest, in Exod. 1:11). Since the Temple was a re-creation of their experience at Sinai, we must conclude that the expression "Church" originally had some association with the Temple and its mysteries. This is particularly true in the Qumran Community, which withdrew into the desert to "make straight the way of the Lord" (Isa. 40:3), a technical expression meaning "to be instructed in the mysteries" (1QS 9:18-20; 8:12-16; compare also Ex. 3:18; 8:1; 10: 25-26; etc., where the object of the Exodus was to participate in the sacrificial cultus).

This "Church" in the wilderness was organized along the same lines adopted by the Christians: "In the Council of the Community there shall be twelve men and three priests, perfectly versed in all that is revealed of the Law. They shall preserve the faith in the Lord with steadfastness and meekness and shall atone for sin by the practice of justice and by suffering the sorrows of affliction" (1QS 8:1-4).

Over every "camp" was a supervisor (mebaqqer) a term corresponding to Greek episkopos, "bishop" (1QS 6:20; CD 14:7-11; 13:7-16). These men were to be priests or sons of Aaron (1QS 9:7; CD 14:6-7), just as in Mormonism (Doct. and Cov, 107:765. All property was held in common (cf. Acts 2:44; 4:32), and all were instructed to love their brethren with special devotion--though the "sons of evil" remained their enemies (cf. John 8:44).

We have already mentioned the dualism of Qumran, which reappears in the Fourth Gospel. "It will be noted", points out Raymond E. Brown, "that not only the dualism but its terminology is shared by John and Qumran" (Anchor Bible, John, N.Y., 1966, lxii). Both therefore considered themselves to be "sons of Light", who were in opposition to the rest of the world, or the "sons of Darkness" (1QS 3:13--4:26; 1QM passim; of. John 3:19-21; 8:42-44; Col. 1:13). The writer of Matthew also claimed that "if thine eye be single, thy whole body shall be full of light. But if thine eye be evil, thy whole body shall be full of darkness" (6:23).

The concept of continuing revelation--so important to Mormonism--is also attested in the Dead Sea Scrolls, proving once and for all that prophecy did not cease with Malachi. According to the "Hymn Scroll", God still revealed himself to the "Teacher of Righteousness": "I give thanks to Thee, Adonai, for Thou hast illumined my face by Thy Covenant...I sought Thee...and like true dawn at daybreak Thou hast appeared unto me" (1QH 4:5-6). Jean Danielou has proposed that this hitherto unknown individual be counted among the great figures of Israel's prophetic tradition. The continuing need for prophets also reappears in the Church's Didache (early 2nd century), which says of bishops, "unto you they also perform the service of prophets and teachers" (15:1).

These are only a few of the important ideas from the Dead Sea Scrolls that are critical for our understanding of the Primitive Church. Danielou has summarized their extreme significance as follows: "By informing us of the immediate environment in which Christianity came into being, the Qumran discoveries resolve a considerable number of problems which exegesis had not been able to solve...The utilization of all these documents, and the comparisons to which they will lead, will doubtlessly considerably augment the number of solved enigmas. It can therefore be said that this is the most sensational discovery ever made" (Les Manuscrits de Is Mar Morte et les Origines du Christianisme, Paris, 1957, 123).

Though we cannot presently show how much older than Qumran these important parallels were, they at least agree in principle with the Book of Mormon's claim that "Christian" doctrines were known before Christ ("Notwithstanding we believe in Christ, we keep the Law of Moses", 2 Nephi 25:24). The Qumran versions of Isaiah (ca. 200 B.C.) also agree in surprising ways with the passages quoted in the Book of Mormon (see Hugh Nibley, Since Cumorah, Salt Lake City, 1967, 127-52). The Dead Sea Scrolls, in short, prove conclusively that "Christianity" had historical precedents, a fact which (contrary to Ms. Layton's quotations on p, 48 of her booklet) did cause considerable consternation amongst Christians when they first appeared.

As Krister Stendahl recalls this early shock, Christians were "badly prepared to receive the good news from the Qumran Scrolls" (The Scrolls and the New Testament, N.Y., 1957, 1). This was because so many believers like Marcion of old "wanted Christianity to be a new religion, just as it is to us" (ibid. 6).

Many feared that "the very foundations of the Christian faith might well be shaken by the realization that a hitherto unknown pre-Christian Jewish religious community had possessed similar beliefs and practices. On such a view Christianity would have to abandon its claim to uniqueness" (R. K. Harrison, The Dead Sea Scrolls, N.Y., 1961, 102).

Such early reactions to the discovery of the Qumran texts undoubtedly contrib- uted to John Allegro's famous article in Harper's Magazine, complaining that the texts were for years given a kind of "deep-freeze" treatment because of their threat to orthodox Christian beliefs (Aug. 1966, p. 46ff. See also Edmund Wilson, The Dead Sea Scrolls, N.Y., 1969,127ff, for more of the controversy surrounding this issue).

Nowadays, mature reflection has decided that Christianity really was "'old', in accordance with the expectations of the prophets" (Stendahl, op. cit., 6), just as the Book of Mormon suggests. In fact, Primitive Christianity claimed to be the oldest religion of all, "the first true religion" (Eusebius, History 1.4). With this in mind, we desire now to draw upon material much older than the Dead Sea Scrolls, material which was to be of great significance in the formation of various doctrines found in the Nag Hammadi texts, just as it is of importance for an understanding of the Mormon claim to represent the Eternal Gospel.

On page 22 of her booklet, Ms. Layton scolds Brother Erickson for his use of Nag Hammadi texts in support of the Mormon doctrine of a Heavenly Mother.

"Mr. Erickson is quite mistaken in his comparison of the L.D.S. heavenly mother with that of Nag Hammadi", she says. "As it has already been explained, there is a female counterpart to the great unknown Father, the great invisible Spirit of Nag Hammadi. She is the Holy Spirit who gives life to all who emanate from her. Elohim is not her spouse. Elohim is the Gnostic creator god of the Old Testament who is in fact Satan, the abortion of darkness."

Unfortunately, Ms. Layton's explanation of "what the Gnostics really believed" is vastly oversimplified, and fails again to recognize the presence of ancient traditions which have been woven together in typical Gnostic fashion. Rather than dismiss them as utterly "non-Mormon", as does Ms. Layton, we need to untangle the confused threads and see where they lead.

In a single paragraph, Ms. Layton has unwittingly touched upon a complex of beliefs ranging from polytheism to the existence of a Mother Goddess, as well as the confused identities of "Father", "Son", "Elohim" and Creator-God, the latter becoming the object of anti-Jewish deprecation. Before going into details, the following general features of this Gnostic "melange" should be noted. (Each number is treated more fully, beginning with the next section):

1-The Nag Hammadi texts contain obvious recollections of an earlier polytheism, which can be traced all the way back to Semitic prehistory. At the head of the original pantheon were a Triad of Father, Mother and Son, which was also the model for Gnostic and Kabbalistic "pantheons".

2-The separate identities of "Father" and "Creator" are maintained, though their names have long been confused, as in the OT. Some of the steps in this scrambling process have been recently elucidated--including the adoption of Trinitarianism, with its theory of "separate yet identical" personalities.

3-The belief in a Mother Goddess--itself an important feature of the Semitic Triad-- has been assimilated by the Gnostics to the third member of the Christian Triad. Thus, the earlier Triad of Father-Mother-Son has been identified with Father-Son-Holy Spirit, with the result that the "Mother" and "Holy Spirit" appear to be the same.

4-As we shall show later, the belief in married pairs of gods (syzygies) led to a corresponding belief in the necessity of human marriage. We will in fact find that there was an ancient pattern, which survived many millennia, recognizing the analogy between divine marriages and their human imitations. What the gods did, man and woman were commanded to do also.

To properly understand these historical developments, it is necessary that we first determine what the early ancestors of Israel believed. This is consistent with the Primitive Church's assertion that God had already revealed himself many times to former generations. If this is true, we should expect to find surviving fragments of this early teaching amongst the ancestral Hebrews.

31

What, then, does history teach us about the oldest known Israelite religion?

1-POLYTHEISM. Originally, there was "no kind of 'El' monotheism among the early Western Semites and in particular among the early Hebrews" (William F. Albright, FSAC, 246-7).

Even Yahwism was not originally an explicit monotheism, but rather a "monar-chism" which tolerated no rivals (Theodore Vriezen, The Religion of Ancient Israel, London, 1967, 35, 12). "The existence of other gods is not denied in the first commandment of the decalog itself; in fact it presupposes their existence and for-bids the Israelites to worship them" (Roland de Vaux, The Early History of Israel, Philadelphia, 1968, 463).

The OT therefore asks: "Who among the gods is like unto thee, Yahweh?" (Ex. 15:11), The Yahwist's obvious answer was, "Now I know that Yahweh is greater than all the gods" (18:11). (Compare also 1 Cor. 8:5-6; Isa. 43:11; 45:21.)

Consequently, "it is today more generally agreed that the religion of the patriarchs is properly to be designated as polytheistic" (Herbert G. May, "The Patriarchal Idea of God", Journal of Biblical Studies 60, 1944, 114). Thus, when Elohim (a plural form "which echoes ancient polytheism"; B. W. Anderson, Interpreter's Bible II:413) says, "Let us make man in our image ", we are hearing in demythologized-form the speech of the Gods in the ancient pantheon, as they discuss the begetting of man (Albright, Yahweh and the Gods of Canaan [YGC), N.Y., 1968, 192; FSAC 369).

The OT is filled with such "debris" from an earlier religious culture (Albright, YGC, 185), which was overwhelmingly polytheistic (cf. Gen. 3,5, 22; 6:2-4; LXX Deut. 32:8; Josh. 24:14; Pa. 82:1; etc.). The OT "sons of God" were the lesser deities of this polytheism, who survived in monotheism as "angels" (Interpreter's Dictionary of the Bible IV:426; Marvin Pope, Anchor Bible, Job, N.Y., 1965, 9). Together with El and Yahweh, they comprised the so-called "Council in Heaven", or SOWD (Albright, [YGC], 191-3; J. Wheeler Robinson, op. cit., 151-7).

At the head of this ancient SOWD was the divine Triad, i.e. the Father, Mother and Son. This Triad has been investigated extensively by such writers as D. Nielsen ("Ras Shamra Mythologie und biblische Theologie", Abhandlungen für die Kunde des Nor-genlandes, Bd. 2, #4, 2; "Die Muttergöttin in Kansan", Zeitschrift der Deutschen Morgenländischen Gesellschaft, 1938, 526-51); Julian Morgenstern (Sono Significant Antecedents of Christianity, Leiden, 1966, 82ff; 96); Maria Hofner Die vorislamitischen Religionen Arabiens, Stuttgart, 1970, 245-6); and Wm. Albright (FSAC, 173, 247).

Writing on the Hebrew version of the Triad, the last author concludes that there was "a father, El, a, mother whose specific name or names remain obscure (perhaps Elat or Anath), and a son who appears as the storm-god, probably nomad Shaddai, 'the One of the Mountain(s)'" (FSAC, 247). The name "Shaddai", of nurse, appears throughout the CT as one of Yahweh's epithets (KJV "God Almighty"), indicating that he was Once considered to be a son of El (Elohim), Statues of the divine Triad have been discovered by Kathleen Kenyon at Jericho, from as early as a. 5000 B.C.

Father - Mother
Son - Son's Wife

Raphael Patai has recently shown that the Triad was often extended into a Tetrad, because the Son--like the Father--was also joined by a wife. Thus, we end up with a pattern of Father-Mother-Son-Son's Wife, perpetuating the original relationship into successive generations. This dynamic Tetrad appears ubiquitously throughout the Near East along aids of the original Triad (The Hebrew Goddess, N.Y., 1967, 164-70). That such a polytheistic conception actually existed in Early Israel--where it survived for many millennia--is proven by the fact that medieval Jews still retained it as an important part of their Kabbalistic belief (ibid., 157-85), with the added explanation that the four letters of the Tetragrammaton YHWH secretly correspond to a heavenly Tetrad of Father-Mother-Son-Son's Wife (ibid., a. 2-4).

The immemorial Triad or Tetrad also reappeared in Christian Gnosticism, where they became the basis for the generations of Aeons descended from the Unknown Father (H. M. Schenke, "Nag Hemadi Studien III", Zeitschrift für Religions- und Geisteages-ohichte, 1962, 352-61). There again the divine offspring of an original Triad sustain the familial pattern in a series of married pairs (syzygies), each with its own offspring. [Compare also the Phoenician divine succession, recorded by Sanchuniathon and Philo Byblis Hesiod's Theogony; the Hurrian succession (in Marvin Pope, El in the Ugaritic Texts, 1955, 56); and the Biblical Triad (in Julian Morgenstern, "The Divine Triad in Biblical Mythology", Journal of Biblical Literature 64, 1945, 15-37; Della Vida, "El Elyon in Genesis", JBL, 1-9).7

The most important connection between the Semitic, Tetrad and the Gnostic syzygies is that the Father's wife (Asherah) was the original model for the Gnostic's higher Sophia, whereas the Son's wife (Ashtoreth-Anath) was the model for the lower Sophia, or the consort of the Savior.

2-EL AND YAHWEH. At the head of all the Semitic pantheons was the great Father "El", "Il", "Ila", etc. (J.J.M. Roberts, The Earliest Semitic Pantheon, Baltimore, 1972, 32, 34). El's Hebrew name was usually given in the majestic plural as "Elohim". In most pantheons, El tended to be otiose; hence, a younger god--generally his son--served as "executive" power in his stead, and as active agent of Creation. Thus, Proverbs 30:4 asks rhetorically concerning the two Creators, "What is His name and what is the name of His son?" (compare also Heb. 1:2).

Otto Eissfeldt ("El and Yahweh", Journal of Semitic Studies 1, 1956, 25-3?), T.J. Meek (University of Toronto Quarterly, 1939, 196), J.A. Emerton ("The Origin of the Son of Man Imagery", Journal of Theological Studies 9, 1958, 240-2), and many others, have convincingly demonstrated that the Israelite El (Elohim) was "an entity different from...and superior to Yahweh" (Eissfeldt, 27). This explains why early Israelite religion could be so easily confused with the Canaanite, which also had a Father-and Son pair, El and Baal.* As a result, the Hebrew Yahweh was often called "Baal" (cf. the name Bealiah, "Baal is Ya", 1 Chron. 12:5; also Hos. 2:16), and early Yahwist kings actually employed Baal-names for their offspring (Interpreter's Dictionary of the Bible 2:842).

*Baal, formerly "son of Dagon", became naturalized in the Canaanite pantheon as "son of El" (Baal Epic II AB 1:5-6; iv:46; IV AB D:5-6; I AB iv:42-3; etc.). Thus, the necessary "Father-Son" paradigm was preserved.

33

Baal

Cyrus H. Gordon has recently cited evidence that El and Yahweh were known as Father and Son in the Ras Shamra tablets, ca. 1400 B.C.

"We now know that the latter is the former's son", he writes, "for in Ugaritic (text ant:pl. X, IV:14) El (the short form of Elohim) declares 'the name of my son is Yawe-El' (the short form of Yahweh Elohim)" (addendum to Before Columbus, N.Y., 1973 edition, 169), Roland de Vaux adds that "the reading has been disputed, but it is certain" (The Early History of Israel, 341), This translation is also supported by A, Herdner (Corpus des tablettes en cuneiforme alphabetique, Paris, 1963, 4) and J. Aistleitner (Wörterbuch der ugaritischen Sprache, Leipzig, 1965, no. 1151). Gordon therefore concludes with the remark, "it is safe to predict a revolution in biblical studies" (op. cit., 169).

Evidence of this same relationship has been demonstrated in the OT by other scholars. The original of Deut, 32:8, for example, clearly shows that El and Yahweh were originally quite separate and distinct, "When the Most High (El Elyon) divided to the nations their inheritance, when he separated the sons of Adam, he set the bounds of the people according to the number of the sons of God; Yahweh's portion is his people, Jacob the lot of his inheritance." The present Masoretic text has altered "sons of God" to "sons of Israel"; but the Septuagint and a recently discovered text from Qumran confirm the earlier reading.

Early Christian versions of Deut. 32:8-9 also show that Elohim and Yahweh were once believed to be separate and distinct. The Clementine Homilies, for example, makes Yahweh both "Son" and "Lord" to whom the "Most High" gave the Hebrews as his portion. The Clementine Recognitions likewise describes the "sons of God" as arch-angels, chief of whom is Christ. This is significant because Pseudo-Cyprian (De centisma sexigisma tricesma) declares that this "chief archangel" was the same One whom Isaiah called "Lord of hosts", i.e. Yahweh (e.g. Isa. 3:1). As we shall presently see, the identification of Christ and Yahweh was widespread in the Primitive Church:

In short, even the present Bible preserves remnants of a very ancient Israelite belief that the Father Elohim, and his Son, Yahweh, were separate and distinct, in direct contradiction to the conspicuous polemic, "Hear, O Israel, Yahweh our Elohim is one Yahweh" (Deut. 6:4).

It is generally acknowledged that when the Patriarchs entered Palestine, they saw in the Canaanite El their own "God of the fathers" (Eissfeldt, op. cit., 30-34). In the same fashion, those Israelites who returned from the experience at Sinai saw in El's son Baal their own Yahweh. Thanks to these correspondences, we have still more evidence that the Israelite El must have been looked upon as "different from... and superior to Yahweh", just as the Canaanite El and Baal, indicating "a monarchic status of El, superior to that of other gods and, among them Yahweh" (ibid., 29).

A comparison of Baal and Yahweh further shows that these two had many personal traits in common. Both were gods of the storm, who "rode upon the clouds" for a "chariot", and whose homes were at the tops of sacred mountains. Both were objects of hieros games cults (OT "whoredoms"), and were accordingly symbolized as bulls.

There is even evidence that Yahweh, like Baal, was once considered to be a dying and resurrecting god, that he too was "thought to pass into the nether world at the appropriate time of the solar year, there to abide for a brief time and to rise victorious over his natural enemy Sheol or Mot or Hameshit, 'The Destroyer'--as he seems to have been entitled in Jerusalem parlance" Julian Morgenstern, "'Son of Man' of Daniel 7:13f', Journal of Biblical Literature 80, 1961, 70-71).

This evidence has found wide acceptance amongst Scandinavian and British scholars of the so-called "Myth and Ritual School". S.H. Hooke, for example, notes how "in Christian apocalyptic this fundamental element in the ancient pantheon re-turns...The conception of a dying and rising god, banished from Jewish thought had survived in the Mystery religions and became the clue to the whole drama in Christian apocalyptic" (The Siege Perilous, London, 1956, 181).

MONOTHEISM, One of the chief goals of the Mosaic reform was the elimination of this ancient pantheon, It was not aimed so much at polytheism itself as against the depravity of sexual worship (hieros games, "Sacred Marriage") connected with the gods and their spouses (Albright, FSAC, 208), In the process, "the traits of the father-god and El were attached to Yahweh" (Vriezen, op. cit., 165). As a result, "the God of Abraham, Isaac and Jacob, in spite of the differences in the names, was identified in his essence with Yahweh" (Eissfeldt, op. cit., 35). Thanks to the merging of these two gods into one, El came to be thought of simply "as a revelation in the past of the God who manifested Himself later under His real name of Yahweh" (ibid., 36).

As younger gods, both Yahweh and Baal had been subject to El, whose character-istics included the titles "King" and "Begetter", par excellence (Roberts, op. cit., 32-4, 94-.6), But after the fusion of El and Yahweh, El's title "King" pass on to the new "Yahweh-Elohim" (KJV "LORD God"), along with his paternal attributes,. ab bn nil "Father of the gods", and ab adm, "Father of men".

"Yahweh-Elohim" now declares his intention to be "father" to Israel (2 Sam. 7:4). As the great "Begetter", he still opens the wombs of Sarah, Rebecca and Leah (Gen. 21:1; 25:21; 29:23), and "begets" royal "sons of God" (Ps. 2:7).

Even El's wife Asherah, passed on to "Yahweh-Elohim", becoming fused in her own turn with the younger god's spouse, Anath-Ashtoreth. Thus, the composite god was married to a composite spouse, who henceforth appeared under three interchange-able names: Asherah, Anath and Ashtoreth (see Patai, op. cit., 29-100).

Just how these original polytheistic ideas--particularly those of a Father and Son, and the dying and rising god--were transmitted from the period of the Monarchy to Christianity remains a mystery (see J.A. Emerton, op. cit., 241-2), unless, of course, they were genuine articles of revealed religion, But the surprising thing is that they did reappear, as both Scripture and the newly discovered sources demonstrate. The official Yahwists by then denied that their God was ever a dying and rising God, like those of their neighbors; Yahweh was strictly a "living God", But the truth was revealed once again in the person of Jesus Christ, the Son, who had the power to lay down his life and take it up again (John 10:18).

As the non-canonical sources in particular reveal, these ancient Semitic ideas also resurfaced in other ways, as well, The Father-Son dichotomy, for instance, became responsible for the doctrine of the inferior Demiurge, that OT Creator who arrogantly believed himself to be the only God, whereas he was in fact subordinate to the Unknown Father (Apocryphon of John II.11,20; Hypostasis of the Archons II. 86:29-30; etc.). As indicated before, this doctrine was due in part to the anti-Jewish bias which developed in the new Church, sometime between 70 and 90 A.D. The fact that many Christians no longer recognized the CI Yahweh as the highest God could now be turned against the Jewish Deity. As Creator of the physical world, he became the object of Gnostic hatred, the Artificer of all that is opposed to the spirit.

Because El and Yahweh had been combined into a single person, however, made it possible for the Demiurge to sometimes appear under the name of "Elohim", as he does in Justin's book, Baruch, or in the particular system mentioned by Ms, Layton (p. 22 of her booklet). But this is a corruption of El's original status of high God. In his true character, El was indeed the husband of Asherah, the real Heaven Mother, who became the archetype for the higher Sophia of Gnosticism. Thus, we are able to correct another error of Ms. Layton, who takes one Gnostic system to be indicative of them all.

The resurgence of polytheism in Primitive Christianity is best exemplified by the Triad of Father, Son and Holy Spirit. Another complication, however, enters the picture here, for it was the belief of an important part of the original Church that Christ himself was the Creator of the OT (John 1:3; 1 Cor. 8:6; 2 Cor. 4,6; Col. 1:15-20; Heb. 1:2).

1 Cor. 10:4 thus identifies Jesus as the "Rock" (Yahweh) who led Moses and Israel through the Red Sea (cf. also Strack and Billerbeck, Kommentar zum Neuen Testament aus Talmud und Midrasch III:408). Acts 4:11 also identifies him as the "Stone" Yahweh refused by the builders, but destined to become "chief cornerstone" of salvation (Ps. 118:22). Writers such as Eusebius (History I.2) plainly state that Jesus was the same Yahweh who communicated with Moses from the Burning Bush, Even the name "I AM", given by Yahweh at that time (Ex. 3:14), was the same name used by Jesus when revealing himself as God of the storm (Ego eimi, "I AM"; **Matt.** 14:27). (Compare also Isa, 43:13 with Mk. 14:62; Lk. 22:70; 24:39 and John 6:20; 8:58. Raymond E. Brown has discussed "I AM" at length in his John, 535-38.) Note also the "Be not afraid!" formula, often associated with "I AM" (Isa. 35:4; Matt. 14:27; John 6:20).

Yahweh's other titles, which were used for Christ, were "the First and the Last" (Isa. 41:4; 44:6; 48:12; Rev, 1:8, 11, 17; 21:6; 22:13; etc.), "Savior" (yasha'; Judg. 3:9, 15; Isa. 45:15, 21; etc.), "Redeemer" (go'el; Job. 19:5; Isa. 43:3; 49:26; etc.). Matt. 3:3 and the other Gospels also declare that Christ is the "Lord", whose way was prepared in the wilderness, as prophesied of Yahweh in Isa. 40:3 and Mal. 3:1. The LXX had already used Kyrios ("Lord") as a translation for YHWH, and the Greek writers of the NT unhesitatingly chose the same word for Jesus. Thus, "to an early Christian accustomed to reading the OT, the word 'Lord', when used of Jesus, would suggest his identification with the God of the OT" (Interpreter's Dictionary of the Bible III:151).

Jesus also assumed the prerogatives of Yahweh when he claimed to forgive sin (Mk. 2:10; cf. Isa, 43:25), or to judge mankind (Matt. 10:32f; John 5:22, 29ff; 9:35; cf. Gen. 15:14; 1 Chron. 16:33; Ps. 96:13). It was in fact because he made himself "equal to God" (John 5:18) that he was eventually put to death.

Yet there is confusion in the NT itself over the true identity of the "Lord Jesus Christ" (Phil. 2:11), for the Yahwist claim that Yahweh and Elohim were "one Yahweh" was eventually brought into the Church by Jews who clung to their traditional monotheism. (See, for example, Mk. 12:29, which puts Deut. 6:4 into the mouth of Jesus: also Acts 3:13; 5:30; 22:14, which declare Jesus' "Lord" to be the "God of our Fathers"; and Matt. 15:31; Lk. 1:68; Acts 13:17, which make him the "God of Israel".)

Whether these reflected Jesus' own belief at an early stage of his development, or were a later assumption on the part of his Jewish converts, cannot presently be answered. But it is perhaps significant that Jesus' own personal prayers were not addressed to "Adonai" (or other legal equivalents of YHWH), but to "El" (Matt. 27:6; Mk. 15:34), or simply to "Abba", the Aramaic word for "Daddy". It is this "Abba that underlies every reference to "Father" in Christ's prayers (e.g. Lk. 11:2ff).

The ultimate solution to this confusion of identities--in which Jesus is both the Son of "Yahweh-Elohim" (Mk, 12:29) and Yahweh himself--was the development of Trinitarianism, which allowed all three members of the Godhead to be the same person. Such a solution had to be found, inasmuch as the totality of Scripture, if accepted literally, would have made Jesus his own Father!

Nevertheless, historical research reveals that Trinitarianism appeared no earlier than the end of the 2nd century.

"The NT does not contain the developed doctrine of the Trinity.'*The Bible lacks the express declaration that the Father, the Son and the Holy Spirit are of equal essence and therefore in an equal sense God himself"* (italics added; The New International Dictionary of New Testament Theology, Grand Rapids, 1976, II:84). The presently "orthodox" concept of the Trinity had to wait until the writings of Athenagoras, ca. 177 A.D., who used the philosophy of Middle Platonism to formulate a doctrine of the metaphysical oneness of God and his Son.

The word trinitas likewise did not appear until Tertullian's Against Praxeas, 3, 11, 12 (ca. 210 A.D.); and the doctrine of homoousios, "one in substance", was not promulgated until Nicea, 325 A.D. Nor may we "imagine that the doctrine of the Trinity such as we have found in Athenagoras' writings had always existed in the Christian subconscious" (R.M. Grant, The Early Christian Doctrine of God, University of Virginia, 1966, 95). The Primitive Church was simply content "to know that there is a Triad of Father, Son and Holy Spirit. They were not concerned with interrelations; at any rate, no such concern is expressed in their extant writings" (ibid. 85), (Note that 1 John 5:7 is an interpolation from as late as the 4th century; Interpreter's Dictionary of the Bible IV:871).

3-THE HEAVENLY MOTHER. There is quite a bit of mystery still surrounding the transmission of belief in a Mother-Goddess from ancient Israel to the time of Christianity. Nevertheless, it is evident that certain elements within the Church were acquainted with the Semitic Triad of Father-Mother-Son, for the Gnostic Christians assimilated it to the canonical Triad of Father-Son-Holy Spirit, with the result that the ancient Goddess was identified with the person of Sophia, the Holy Spirit.

The existence of Mariolatry in Catholicism has long been cited as evidence that the Primitive Church was acquainted with the Mother Goddess. Indeed, it was the latter's title, "Queen of Heaven" (Jer. 7:18; 44:18), which reemerged as Mary's epithet, Regina Coeli.

E.G. James has shown that the Great Mother survived amongst Israel's neighbors' right down to the time of Christianity (The Cult of the Mother Goddess, N.Y., 1959, 161-227). But there is also evidence that her memory was already part of Jewish tradition.

To begin with, the OT repeatedly refers to the existence of her cult, though retrospectively anathematized and declared a "pagan" importation. Her worship can actually be documented as late as the 5th century B.C. at Elephantine, Upper Egypt, where a Jewish garrison was stationed. This was the very worship which generations of prophets had striven to eradicate, beginning with Hosea (ca. 800 B.C.), who proposed that Israel celebrate her covenant "marriage" to Yahweh instead of the "adulterous" nuptials of the Goddess: "Plead with your mother (Israel), plead...She is no longer my wife, neither am I her husband. Let her therefore put away her whoredoms out of her sight" (Hos. 2:2). Israel should henceforth "abide with me (Yahweh) for many days; thou shalt not play the harlot, and thou shalt not be for another man; so will I also be for thee...and it shall be in that day that thou shalt can me Ishi ('husband')" (3:3; 2:11).

Later prophets not only continued to speak of Yahweh's covenant with Israel as a "marriage", but described it in terms of an allegorical hieros gamos, showing that the literal nuptials of the Goddess and her Husband lay behind the entire conception: "Now when I passed by thee and looked upon thee, behold thy time was the time of love; and I spread my skirt over thee, and covered thy nakedness" (Ezek. 16:8). Jeremiah referred to this union as "the love of thine espousals, when thou wentest after me in the wilderness (Jer. 2:2). Any return to the worship of the Goddess would henceforth be viewed as "adultery", for Israel was now the legitimate "wife" of Yahweh (Isa. 54:6).

But the OT could never completely eliminate references to the former Wife, a divine Mother who bore real offspring, as did Asherah, the wife of E called Qaniyatu 'elima, "She Who Gives Birth to the Gods", in the Ras Shamra tablets. There, she was described as the Mother of the 70 "sons of God" (= "Stars of Morning"; Job 38:7), the celestial counterpart of the Israelite "70", or the ideal number of the earthly Community (cf. Ex. 1:5), and the heavenly SOWD.

Since the number "70" frequently alternates with a more compact "7"--especially in writings of Mesopotamian provenance--we find parallel sources describing the Goddess as Mother of the "7 sons of God", i.e. the "planets" or "cosmic pillars" (Prov. 9:1; Jer. 15:9).

In still other sources she becomes the Mother of "12", corresponding to the divine ancestors of the 12 Tribes of Israel. As such, she is the source of the astral pantheon after

38

which Jacob's earthly family is patterned (Gen. 37:9-10). In the NT she appears directly as a Mother "crowned with 12 stars" (Rev. 12:1-2; of. also 21:2, 12-14).

This "Mother of young men" (Jer. 15:8)--whether "7", "12" or "70"--was obviously a child-bearing Goddess in her original form. In Jer. 31:15, she is the "Mother Rahel", weeping for her children. In the LXX of Ps. 87:5, and in Isa. 66:8, she becomes the "Mother Zion", or Progenitress of Israel. In later apocalypses, such as 4 Ezra 7:10, and in the NT (Gal. 4:25), she is described as the "Mother of us all". In all of these passages, her assimilation to the Community of Israel is nearly complete.

But in the last examples, she also becomes identified with the pre-existent Community, showing that a fresh impetus has been given to the use of the Goddess symbol, In short, Man's heavenly origin is again being stressed, suggesting once more the phenomenon of natural birth in the celestial realms.

One already finds hints of the Goddess as Mother of the Divine Son (Rev. 12:5) in pre-Christian Judaism. In early Israelite religion she had been Mother of "Shaddai", or KJV "God Almighty" (Albright, FSAC, 247). Her role as Mother of the Creator must have survived for several millennia, as demonstrated by the fact that in Christianity she was still "Mother of God", and in Gnosticism, "Mother" of Ialdaboth, the Demiurge (George MacRae, "The Jewish Background of the Gnostic Sophia Myth", Novum Testamentum 12, 1970, 88).

Isaiah's well-known prophecy, "Behold a virgin (almah) shall conceive and bear a Son, and shall call his name Immanuel" (7:14), has also been cited as evidence of this same belief, for the word almah ("mature young woman of child-bearing age") is historically connected with the cult prostitutes (almoth) who impersonated the Great Mother in the Israelite hieros gamos cult (Beatrice A. Brooks, "Fertility Cult Functionaries in the OT", JBL 66, 1941, 242). Her sign was the dove (Erich Neumann, The Great Mother, N.Y., 1955, 311, 141), the very symbol used in the NT to denote the presence of the Holy Spirit (Matt. 3:14). In the Protoevangelium, the Virgin Mary "continued in the Temple as a dove" (8:2), showing that a connection existed even then in the minds of Christians between Christ's Mother, the Holy Spirit, and this ancient symbol of the Great Mother.

(One should also recall that Anath, one of Goddess's OT names, was always described in the Ras Shamra texts as btlt, "the Virgin", i.e. one who is eternally fecund.)

The Dead Sea Scrolls (1QH 3:8ff) also describe "a woman pregnant with her first child, a male. After terrible pains she gives birth to the 'marvelous counselor' (the description of the promised king in Isa ix 5[6])" (Raymond E. Brown, John, 731).

Dupont Sommer interprets this as pre-Christian evidence of the myth which appears in Rev. 12, where the Mother gives birth supernaturally to the divine Messiah (The Essene Writings from Qumran, Oxford, 1961, 208). She is the same Mother whom we saw in Prov. 9:1 as "Sophia, who hath built her house of seven pillars", and Jer. 15:9, "she who hath borne seven sons"; for in early Christian thought, the preexistent Church consisted ideally of seven archangels, chief of whom was Christ, the Divine Son (Danielou, Theology of Jewish Christianity, 166-72, 299-301).

This doctrine is further alluded to in the writings of Clement of Alexandria, Anastasius Sinaites and Papias, who claimed that they had it orally from the Apostles themselves (Danielou, ibid.). In the Shepherd of Hermas, the pre-existent Church appears as an Old Woman, or a "Tower", builded by seven, i.e. "six young men and the Lord" (V. III.3:3ff). The "Old Woman's" original identity as the Great Mother was curiously reaffirmed when the Catholic Church taught that Mary--her earthly counter-part--was "assumed" back into heaven, where she came from in the first place!

The Mother-Goddess continued to appear throughout the Nag Hammadi texts under a variety of names, most of which have to do with Wisdoms i.e. "Sophia", ennoia ("thought"), the "Great Sophia", "Pro-Gnosis" ("Foreknowledge"), "Achamoth" (= Hebrew chochmah, "Wisdom"), "Barbelo" (= Hebrew Barbhe Eloha, "in the four [the Tetrad] is God"), etc. According to the researches of Hans-Martin Schenke ("Nag Hamadi Studiem III"), all of these Gnostic Sophias were derived from the Mother of an original Triad which corresponds exactly to the Semitic Triad, i.e. the Father, his wife, Sophia-Barbelo, and their common Son, Christus (ibid., 361).

In the Gospel of Philip, the Mother "Sophia" is the true Heavenly Mother of both Christ and the Church, Saying 82, for example, tells us that Christ originated in the heavenly Bridal Chamber, from a union of the "Father of the All" and the "virgin who came down." Saying 55 refers to her as "Sophia whom they call 'barren', the Mother of the angels". And she is our mother too: "Through the Holy Spirit (Sophia), we are indeed born, but we are reborn through Christ" (Saying 74), The Sophia of Jesus Christ appropriately calls her the "Mother of the universe" (104:19). In still other works, such as the Hypostasis of the Archons and On the Origin of the World, Sophia is the celestial counterpart of Eve, i.e. the heavenly "Mother of all living" (MacRae, op. cit., 93).

But there is also a lower Sophia who is "our sister" (Apocryphon of John II.23:: 20-1; BG 36:16), This emphasizes the fact that the present earthly Community is essentially a "fallen" extension of the Heavenly Mother, for which reason "Sophia-the-Mother" and "Sophia-the-Church" are often indistinguishable (cf. Gal. 4:26; Rev, 21:2). Moreover, it is Christ who refers to the lower Sophia as "our sister", thus stressing his common ancestry with the reader (MacRae, op. cit., 93; of. Heb. 2:11). It is significant that the account of Irenaeus also makes Sophia the "sister" of Christ (Against Heresies I. 30:11-12). Thus, she exactly parallels Anath, the wife of Baal, who was sister of the god before they were married.

Because of the original bi-sexual nature of Semitic pantheons, this lower Sophia could appear either as a "sister" or "brother", Certain elements in the Church therefore understood God's "Wisdom" (= Sophia) to be a pre-existent form of Christ (1. Cor. 1:24; Col. 2:3; Jas. 3:17). Christ was also identified with the Jewish "Word" (John 1:1-14), another manifestation of "Wisdom". This masculine "Wisdom" can be detected in the OT as early as Job 28 or Prov. 1:23ff. 1 Clem. 57:3ff. also describes "Wisdom" as the Savior, who "came unto his own, but his own received him not" (cf. Lk. 11:49ff; 13:34f; Matt, 23:34-39). Here again, we encounter the theme of the "Homeless Wisdom" (cf. the "theology of the Pilgrim", above), who is a literal "Brother" among brethren.

But returning to the feminine "Sophia", it is important to note that nearly all of the ritual appearances of a female goddess in early Israelite sources had to do with the lower Sophia, or consort of the Son. As Patai demonstrates in The Hebrew Goddess, only the nuptials of the younger pair were traditionally celebrated as a hieros gamos (179-80), although a Sacred Marriage was once celebrated by El himself in the Ras Shamra texts (The Birth of the Fair and Gracious Gods). This is extremely important because it helps us to fix the true identities of Yahweh and Christ within the ancient pantheon; both were sons, both were "espoused" to their own brethren, their allegorical "sisters", or "spouses".

The nuptials of the "lesser Sophia" also appear in allegorized form in works such as Wisdom of Solomon, which describes David's son as the royal participant in a spiritualized hieros gamos with the Goddess (8:2). Just why Solomon was chosen to represent the Divine Son and King in this fashion is unknown; but there is evidence that even in early times his name was connected with fertility rites involving the Goddess (William Albright, "Archaic Survivals in the Text of Canticles", Hebrew and Semitic Studies, ed. D.W. Thomas and W.D. McHardy, Oxford, 1963, 1-71 YGC, 148-50 Marvin J. Pope, Anchor Bible, Song of Songs, N.Y., 1977, 432-3; etc.). In rabbinical literature, "Solomon" was one of the secret names of Yahweh, whose Sacred Marriage to Israel is the subject of Song of Songs (Louis Ginzberg, Legends of the Jews VI:277). In another version of Wisdom of Solomon, found at Qumran, the King's hieros gamos is described in considerable erotic detail (T.H. Caster, The Dead Sea Scriptures, 3rd ed., 1976, 481-91).

Philo also developed the startling idea of God's "Wisdom" as a Goddess with whom the believer could have "sexual intercourse", This, of course, was a variation of the allegorical hieros gamos between Yahweh and Israel, only on an individual level. Since God was clearly bi-sexual (Patai, op. cit., 115; E.R. Goodenough, By Light, Light! New Haven, 1935, 248), divine revelation could come through God's feminine aspect, as well as his masculine, which in this case appeared to the husband in the guise of his wife! In the ensuing "divine impregnation", God implants wisdom in the wife, who then represents God's feminine nature to the husband.

De Cherubim 48, for example, tells how Leah's womb was implanted with the "seed of Wisdom" for Jacob; chapters 45 and 50 tell of Sarah's case for Abraham; and 47 tells how Zipporah was found by Moses to be pregnant "through no mortal agency".

According to Philo, these were actually allegories on the way in which the Patriarchs were "impregnated" with the divine Wisdom, for their wives served as intermediaries in the "divine intercourse" with God. In short, the wife became a surrogate for Sophia, receiving the "pure seeds of divinity which the Father of all sows from above" (Goodenough, op. cit., 158). These in turn were conveyed to the husband in the wedding chamber by the wife. Philo describes the complete chain of events in an amazing allegory on the story of Isaac and Rebecca (Quaest, in Gen. 4: 110-46), where Rebecca, who is already impregnated by God with divine "Wisdom", becomes a surrogate for the Mother herself, who dwells thereafter with the righteous couple as long as they observe the holy laws of matrimony (Goodenough, op. cit., 160).

Thus, Philo brought the divine hieros gamos into conjunction with the lesser

41

hieros gamos of the husband and wife, This notion that human intercourse was intimately connected with divine intercourse survived as late as medieval Kabbalism,
where the nuptials of the earthly couple remained a "symbolic reference to the heavenly
marriage" (Gershom Scholem, On the Kabbalah and its Symbolism, N.Y., 1965, 140),
This Sacred Marriage Feast was regularly performed on the Eve of the Sabbath,
demonstrating that what appears on the surface to be mere poetry often conceals realistic
practices of great antiquity. We also recognize here--in allegorical dress--the ancient
concept of "dual paternity", which postulates that every conception involves two fathers,
a human and a divine ("Neither man without woman, nor woman without man, and
neither of them without the Holy Spirit"; Genesis Rabbah 89), for there are always three
partners in the production of a man: "The Holy One, blessed be He, the father and the
mother" (Talmud, Kiddushin 30b; compare also Gen. 21: 1; 25:21; 29:23; cf, 1 Cor,
11:11).

Kabbalistic doctrine therefore decreed that the husband and wife come together
at exactly midnight, Friday, when the "King and Queen" were said to unite above
(Patai, op. cit., 195-6), thus vitalizing human procreation with the procreative act of
God, the literal "Father of Spirits" (cf. Heb). 12:9; Acts 17:28). The timing was
important, for only at the proper moment could the best souls be drawn into the
offspring of the human couple. Such superior offspring were called "Sons of the King"
(A.E. Waite, The Holy Kabbalah, N.Y., 1960, 388).

But the "secret of Divine Generation is...a Secret of the Doctrine and is reserved for the initiated therein; it is apparently they alone who draw down holy souls
who are the fruit of union between God and His Shekhinah" (i.e. his feminine aspect;
ibid. 388).

Thus, we discover one of the important reasons why human pre-existence was
only discussed in secret, for "it is good to keep close the secret of a King in order that the
doctrine of the entrance of souls into bodies may not be thrown before the common
understanding, nor what is holy be given to the dogs, nor pearls before swine" (Origen,
Contra Celsus 5:29). (Presently, we shall reveal an even more surprising reason why the
theology of hierogamy and human pre-existence was reserved for esoteric instruction,)

The Jews began sometime in the first century to call God's "Feminine Aspect"--
who participated with him in the production of souls--"Shekhinah". Although official
monotheism by that time denied that any feminine counterpart of Yahweh literally
existed, the Goddess's immemorial attributes reemerged in the strongly anthropomorphic
figure who was said to be the portion of God that dwells on earth (from sh-ch-n, "to
dwell"). As such, she closely resembles the Holy Spirit, who acted as creative agent when
the worlds were organized (Gen. 1:2), She was also a late form of the divine Presence,
which accompanied Israel in the wilderness (Ex. 33:14), In short, Shekhinah is God's
"female" extension, by which he is present in the world, and through which he manifests
himself to men.

Shekhinah's attributes--derived almost wholly from the ancient Goddess--tell why
she is called "Queen", or "Matronit", in medieval Judaism, and why her sacred nuptials
with the King were still said to provide prosperity and fertility to earthly couples who

imitate them. Even in spite of the intervening monotheism, we still "perceive dimly behind these mystical images the male and female gods of antiquity, anathema as they were to the pious Kabbalist" (Scholem, Major Trends in Jewish Mysticism, N.Y., 1954, 227).

But while monotheistic Jews had to interpret this hierogamy in symbolic fashion, the Nag Hammadi texts show that certain Christians took a more literal view of the Goddess. As we have already seen, there were for them two Sophias, the parent of Christ and the Church, and the Church herself, Christ's "sister", or "spouse", from before Creation.

"According to Irenaeus", Dr. Wilson writes, "the Savior is the bridegroom of Sophia-Achamoth the bride; since Jesus is the Savior, he can hardly have originated from their union. There must therefore have been an earlier union" (op. cit., 147). This "earlier union" could only have been one involving the Father and Mother of Christ. "Because of this, (Christ's) body, which came into being on that day, came out of the (heavenly) Bridal Chamber, in the manner of him who came into being from the bridegroom and the bride" (i.e. the Father and Mother; Gospel of Philip, Saying 82), This certainly was more realistic than the monotheistic Jews would have allowed. In the opinion of Wilson, such passages refer "to natural birth...All men are born through the Holy Spirit (Sophia), but only the Gnostic is reborn 'through Christ" (italics added; op. cit., 137).

This natural birth is attested by other works around 140 A.D. "If you know yourselves, then you will be known and you will know that you are sons of the Living Father, But if you do not know yourselves, then you are in poverty, and you are poverty" (Gospel of Thomas, Legion 3), Irenaeus explains this doctrine as follows: "Son is understood in two ways; First, according to nature, for he was born a son; Second, according to what he became he was considered a Son" (Against Heresies IV, 41:1).

Such a literal understanding of "sons of God", however, must have also existed prior to the 2nd century, for "clearly", write Robert Graves and Raphael Patai, "such an interpretation was still current in the second century A.D., and lapsed only when the Bene Elohim were re-interpreted as 'sons of judges" (italics added; Hebrew Myths, N.Y., 1966, 104).

Thus, Rabbi Shimeon ben Yohai "felt obliged to curse all who read 'Sons of God' in the Ugaritic sense" (i.e. literally), as stated in the Genesis Rabba (ibid., 104), One of the texts upon which this literal understanding was based is Gen. 6: 1-4, which records that the first men were naturally descended from "sons of God". This story reoccurs through apocalyptic texts just prior to Christianity, including the Qumran Book of Giants. Such literal "sonship", of course, requires some sort of Heavenly Mother.

The doctrine that Christ was literally begotten in the flesh by a Heavenly Father also shows that celestial copulation was taken for granted, (See also Lk. 3:38, which states that Adam was the son of God, just as Seth was the son of Adam.

X

4-MARRIAGE DOCTRINE. Those who still oppose the idea of sexual relations in the spiritual realms will be surprised to learn from Raphael Patai's recent research that the Cherubim in the Jerusalem Holy of Holies had sometime in the history of the Second Temple had been redesigned to represent the sexual act itself! (The Hebrew Goddess, 101-36; 300-10).

"In their last version", he writes, "the Cherubim depicted a man and woman in sexual embrace--an erotic representation which was considered obscene by the pagans when they at last had a chance to glimpse it" (ibid., 101).

Evidence from the rabbinic literature proves conclusively that these embracing statues not only existed, but were shown to pilgrims assembled in the Holy Place on the three major feasts of Passover, Weeks and Tabernacles.

According to B. Yoma 54a, "when Israel used to make the Pilgrimage, (the priests) would roll up the veil before the Holy of Holies, and show them the Cherubim which were intertwined with each other." Rashi, writing in the 11th century, recalled that they "were joined together, and were clinging to, and embracing each other, like a male who embraces a female." Rabbi Shimeon ben Laqish added that when strangers finally entered the Sanctuary, "they saw the Cherubim intertwined with each other; they took them out into the market place and said, Israel, whose blessing is a blessing, and whose curse is a curse, should occupy themselves with such things: And they despised her because they had seen her nakedness" (B. Yoma 54b).

Dr. Patai chose to limit his study to the influence of the Goddess on Jewish religion and folklore; but others have begun to uncover important parallels between the Cherubim and their own fields of investigation.

Marvin J. Pope, for example, in 1977 related the contents of the Holy of Holies to the exegesis of Song of Songs (op. cit.; see especially 153-79). Undoubtedly, the Cherubim and Song of Songs were synonymous expressions of the same nuptial doctrine, as Rabbi Akiba's double entendre in the Mishna indicated long ago: "For all the writings are holy, but Song of Songs IS the Holy of Holies" (Yadaim 3:5).

In a book of our own (A Great Mystery, 1979, unpublished), we have applied Dr. Patai's discovery to important problems of Christian theology. It was, for example, the custom in early Christian literature to refer to the Holy of Holies (the entire area behind the veil in early Temples) as a "Bridal Chamber" (e.g. Gospel of Philip, Saying 76). The reason for this is now obvious. And knowing that the Bridal Chamber was a real place, we now have a totally new way of viewing Christ's description of the disciples as "sons of the Bridal Chamber" (Matt. 9:15; etc.), an obvious Semiticism meaning "those who are cultically associated with the Holy of Holies". This shows that the Gnostic "Bridal Chamber rites", so often described in the Nag Hammadi and patristic writings, had their beginnings in the Temple cult itself.

As Josephus suggests (Wars 6:301), the "married" Cherubim were called "Bridegroom" and "Bride" in Jerusalem Temple parlance. Thus, we have still another reason why Jesus was accused of equating himself with God, for in taking the name "Bridegroom" upon himself (Matt. 9:15; John 3:29; etc.), he was obviously using an epithet reserved for Yahweh!

The Jews gave us a number of different explanations for the "wedded" Cherubim.

Philo said that they represented the harmony of God's "male" and "female" aspects (De Cherubim 49), or the union of his "creative" and "intellectual" powers, from which the material world was born (On Drunkenness). But even these contrived, philosophical interpretations contain obvious recollections of Israel's former belief in a literal Heavenly Father and Mother, and their hieros gamos.

The rabbis further explained that the Cherubim represented the "marriage" of God and Israel. In this sense, they were visible equivalents of Song of Songs. When the veil of the Temple was rolled up, the priests used to say, "Behold, your love before God is like the love of male and female" (B. Yoma 54a), This explanation was shared by Christianity, making Christ the husband of the new Israel, or the Church.

But the rabbis also taught that the "married" Cherubim portrayed the very image of God, which men and women were commanded to take upon themselves: "He who does not marry thereby diminishes the image of God" (Tosefta, Yebamoth 8:4). This is the same image that was recorded in Genesis: "So God created man in his own image...male and female"(1:27), and to which Adam and Eve were commanded to conform when they "clave together" to become "one flesh" (2:24). This image again recalls Israel's former belief in male and female gods, and their hieros gamos.

It is critically important, then, that the divine model of male-female union be always imitated by the earthly union of husband and wife. Jesus himself strongly reiterated the divine command to marry (Matt. 19:5). And since the most widely revered example of divine "union" was the allegorical "marriage" of God and his people, Paul directly equated the "marriage" of Christ and the Church with the marriage of man and wife (Eph. 5:22-32). Both, he wrote, exemplified the same "Great Mystery" (vs. 32), which is male and female become One. Moreover, if man and woman are to be one with Christ, they must also be one with each other (1 Cor. 11:11). This explains why the Gnostic Bridal Chamber rites simultaneously united both man and woman, and man and Christ, for each symbolizes the other. In this way, the love of the man for his wife becomes "a seal and love-token and eternal symbol" of the divine marriage which it imitates (Baruch, in Hippolytus, Refutations V.26:8).

Ms. Layton is therefore very much in error when she says on p. 17 of her booklet that the marriage celebrated in the Bridal Chamber was only that of Christ and mankind, "not between earthly husband and wife". Informed scholars have long con-ceded that the passage in Gospel of Philip, Saying 77, for example, "'The woman is united to her husband in the Bridal Chamber', is to be understood as the sacrament *taken quite literally*" (italics added; Andrew Helmbold, The Nag Hammadi Gnostic Texts and the Bible, Grand Rapids, 1967, 70). This is because the human union was "some sort of re-enactment of the archetypal situation" (ibid.), just as in Gen. 1:27 and 2:24, and Eph. 5:31-32.

45

"Just as *husband and wife unite* in the bridal chamber, so also the reunion effected by Christ takes place in a bridal chamber, the sacramental, spiritual one, where a person receives a foretaste and assurance of ultimate union with an angelic, heavenly counterpart" (italics added, Wesley Isenberg, in The Nag Hammadi Library, 131).

The "spiritual Bridal Chamber" is, of course, heaven, the celestial counterpart of the earthly Bridal Chamber (Gospel of Philip, Saying 82). There it is that the "fallen" Sophia and her seed will enter in to be joined with Christ and his "angels", the pre-existent counterparts of human souls, at the final hieros gamos of Christ and the Church.

R. McLain Wilson also expresses the opinion that a real marriage took place between man and woman (op. cit., 121), as does Till, one of the German scholars work-ing with the new material (ibid.). "The point would then not be that the Gnostic receives the Savior and Sophia, but that the bridal chamber was the *earthly counterpart* of the final union in the Pleroma" (italics added; ibid.).

That what happens in the Bridal Chamber was therefore both an earthly and a heavenly marriage is stressed several times by Dr. Wilson.

"The 'bridegroom' is the Savior, Sophia the 'bride', and the Pleroma is the archetypal bridal chamber. Of this, *earthly marriage* is the counterpart" (italics added, ibid., 21). "The sacred marriage of the Aeons provided the model for *earthly activity*, and the Valentinian sacrament of the bridal chamber was in some sense a foretaste of the final bliss" (italics added; ibid., 96). For this reason, "to see the Bridegroom and the Bride one must become a bridegroom or a bride" (italics added; ibid., 184), for human beings can only pass through the veil "to the secret of the truth...through despised symbols and weaknesses" (Gospel of Philip, Saying 125).

The "despised symbols" are, of course, the embracing Cherubim, and the "weak-nesses" human marriage. Only those who participate in marriage can pass through the veil (Heb. 10:19-20) to become true "sons of the Bridal Chamber" (Gospel of Philip, Saying 103). And "if anyone becomes a Son of the Bridal Chamber, he will receive the Light. If anyone does not receive it while he is in this world, he will not receive it in the other place"; Saying 127; of. Matt. 22:30) for "the union is in this world man and woman", a "type or image" of the higher "truth" (Gospel of Philip, Sayings 103, 124).

Note also that the Bridal Chamber is described as specifically for "men and virgins" (Saying 73), i.e. for human participants, who are to be united as husband and wife (Saying 79). Saying 122 likewise indicates that "bridegrooms and brides belong to the Bridal Chamber".

While it is true that both Gnostics and medieval Christians eventually aposta-tized from the Savior's true doctrine of marriage (Matt. 19:5)--supposing that only "spiritual marriages" between Christ and the worshipper were of ultimate value--the Gospel of Philip remains "incomparably closer to normative Christianity" (Grobel, op. cit., 15). Later Valentinians, as shown by the Church Fathers, did eventually begin to preach distorted views of marriage; but there is "danger in allowing these known

Valentinian associations to color our exegesis (of the Gospel of Philip)" (Wilson, op. cit., 121). Even Valentinians' pupil Ptolemy still "reveals to us a very 'moderate Gnostic' (Bultmann)...who says nothing that could make one guess the existence of the bizarre speculations of Irenaeus' chapters 1-8" (referring to Against Heresies; Grobel, op. cit., 14).

In short, the true Valentinian doctrine of marriage--as outlined in the Gospel of Philip--is little different from that of Paul in Ephesians. Clement of Alexandria in fact declared (ca, 200 A.D.) that the Valentinians were distinguished from other Gnostics by their warm approval of marriage (Miscellanies III: 1:1 . That they occasionally referred to human union as "unclean" (Gospel of Philip, Saying 122) simply meant that it is presently carnal in contrast to the heavenly marriage to come (Wilson, op. cit., 96). The Naassenes also used this language when they contrasted the "lesser mysteries" of carnal generation with the "greater and heavenly mysteries" (Hippolytus, Refutations V.8:44).

Thus, we may confidently conclude that it was initially necessary for man and woman to participate in the "lesser mysteries" of human marriage before partaking of, the heavenly "union" of Christ and the Church and the reunion of the soul with its pre-existent counterpart (an image of resurrection). Indeed, "whosoever is not in the world and has not loved a woman so as to unite with her, is not of the truth" (Irenaeus, Against Heresies I.6:4). (Compare also the Carpocratians, who believed copulation to be an "ordinance of God"; Clement, Miscellanies 3. 8:2).

Even in Philonic Judaism, the Patriarchs' experiences with their wives were stages in man's ascent up the "ladder of light" (Gen. 28:12) to final union with God (Good-enough, By Light, Light!, 23, 158). The embracing Cherubim therefore appear to have been shown during at least one period to pilgrims who came to the Temple with their wives (Julian Morgenstern, "The Gates of Righteousness". Hebrew Union College Annual, 1927, 28fn.). These undoubtedly received the celestial Wedding Image for guidance in their own affairs, for "he who does not marry thereby diminishes the image of God".

This Jewish doctrine of marriage--particularly Philo's--strongly prefigures the Valentinian, where salvation is experienced in anticipatory fashion in the mystery of the Bridal Chamber (Richard Baer, Jr., Philo's Use of the Categories Male and Female, Leiden, 1970, 68). Goodenough recognized some time ago that this centered about the "mystery of the holy of holies...the mystery of the sacred marriage with Sophia" (op. cit., 250), but he remained unaware of the Cherubim which so graphically represented it. Thanks to Patai's research, however, the complete story of the "Great Mystery" is again becoming visible to Jews and Christians alike, who care to learn what their predecessors really believed. For us, it is additional evidence that the Nag Hammadi doctrine of the Bridal Chamber had legitimate historical antecedents, and was not merely an isolated example of "heresy".

We now have good reason to conclude that the Cherubim represented the Divine Image, or ritual "Face of God", as it was called in the language of the Temple.

The traditional commandment to "appear thrice yearly before the Face of

Yahweh" (Deut. 16:16) should actually read, "see the Face of Yahweh" (ra'ah 'et-pene YHWH); but by changing the qal-form of ra'ah to a niph'al, the verb "see" had been reduced sometime in the past to a more passive "appear" (Walter Eichrodt, Theology of the Old Testament, Engl. Trans. Philadelphia, 1961, II: 35-6). Significantly, it was the Cherubim which were shown on the exact same feast days when the pilgrims were commanded to "see Yahweh's Face"--or the male-female Image of God (Gen. 1:27).

Later, undoubtedly because of its sexual connotation, the expression "Face of Yahweh" was changed to "Face of Shekhinah" (Helmer Ringgren, Israelite Religion, Engl. Trans., Philadelphia, 1966, 163). This is readily understandable, however, when we recall that Shekhinah was none other than the ancient Goddess in demythologized form, and that in Canaanite and early Hebrew sources she was already referred to as the "panim (Face) of God", being the one who was ordinarily visible in the shrines (Albright, YGC, 129-30, 135; FSAC 373). In fact, it was her hieros gamos with Yahweh that was replaced by the wedded Cherubim when polytheism was officially forbidden.

That the Church continued to venerate the Cherubim is shown by the noticeable reticence on the part of the author of Heb. 9:5 to say anything specific about the famous statues, even though he had just described in some detail the other contents of the Holy of Holies:

> And above (the Ark) are Cherubim of glory, overshadowing the mercy seat, concerning which things this is not the proper time to speak in detail (peri on ouk estin nun legein kata meros) (trans. by G.W. Buchanan, Anchor Bible, Hebrews, N.Y.,1972, 89).

This is the very same reticence displayed by Philo and Josephus when obliged to speak of the Holy of Holies (Patai, op. cit. 111-121).

The former declared that the smoke from the High Priest's incense made it impossible to see anything inside (cf. Lev. 16:13). The latter said there was nothing at all to see, though on another occasion he admitted that the contents of the Holy of Holies were "acceptable to piety", even though it was illegal to reveal what they were!

The Gospel of Truth (ca. 140 A.D.) again makes reference to the Cherubim when describing the entry of couples into the Holy of Holies: "Theirs in his head, which becomes a repose for them, and they are enclasped as they approach him, so that they have partaken of his Face by means of the embraces" (i.e. the wedded Cherubim) (41:28-34). This must have also been part of the "Bridal Chamber rites" performed by later Gnostics: "For some of them prepare a Bridal Chamber and perform a mystic rite with those who are being initiated...affirming that it is a spiritual marriage which is celebrated by them in the likeness of unions above" (Irenaeus, Against Heresies 1.21:3). This agrees completely with the statements in Gospel of Philip that "we go in through despised symbols" (Saying 125), and that "the woman is united to her husband in the Bridal Chamber" (Saying 79).

That something realistic occurred is further illustrated by the fact that early Christians felt obliged to defend themselves against accusations of immoral behavior.

48

Justin Martyr, for example, protested that "promiscuous intercourse is not one of our mysteries" (1st Apology 29). Irenaeus, on the other hand, claimed that the rite was not very spiritual at all, for some of the women became pregnant, This report may have only been polemic, however, for (as Bousset observed some years ago) the writer probably no longer understood the true meaning of the ceremony, and saw it as a deception practiced on unwary females (Wilson, op. cit., 21).

H. M. Schenke is of the opinion that the ritual of the Bridal Chamber culminated in a simple kiss ("Das Evangelium nach Phillipus", Theologische Literaturseitung, 1959, 5). This is supported by the Gospel of Philip, which says "the perfect conceive through a kiss and give birth" (i.e. become "sons of God"). "Because of this we kiss one another" (Saying 31). The same document also declares that Jesus kissed Mary Magdalene (his wife!) on the mouth (Saying 55) Eric Segelberg concludes that the sole outward action by which the sacred union was expressed was such a kiss ("The Coptic-Gnostic Gospel According to Philip", Numen, 1960, 198).

According to the Gospel of Philip, those who participated in this Bridal Chamber rite would never again be separated, but have eternal life:

> If the woman had not separated from the man, she would not die with the man. His separation became the beginning of death. Because of this Christ came, in order that he might remove the separation which was from the beginning, and again unite the two, and that he might give life to those who died in the separation and unite them, But the woman is united to her husband in the Bridal Chamber. But those who have united in the Bridal Chamber will no longer be separated (Sayings 78-9).

> When Eve was in Adam, there was no death, but when she separated from him, death came into being. Again, when they reconcile and he receives her to himself, death will be no more (Saying 71).

There must have been a time when Jews and Christians both held this belief, since it reoccurs years later in Jewish Kabbalism, showing that both traditions had a common source:

> A man that does not want to complete the Holy Name here below (by marrying), it were better for him that he were not created, because he has no part in the Holy Name, And when he dies and his soul leaves him, it does not unite with him at all because he has diminished the image of his maker (Zohar III:7a).

The reference to "completing the Holy Name" means that the man and woman "cleave to-gather" and produce sons and daughters, so that the family Tetrad--represented by the Tetragrammaton, YHWH--can be recreated here below, Otherwise.

> He (who) is not both male and female (together) is considered only half a body, No blessing rests upon anything that is blemished or lacking (cf. Deut. 2311); it is found only in that which is complete, in something whole and undivided. A thing which is divided cannot endure forever, nor will it ever

49

receive blessing (Zohar III: 296a).

That the man and woman who have "completed the Holy Name" in this fashion would continue together beyond death was also taught in 1 Enoch--that favorite text of the Primitive Church.

After the Resurrection, it says, "the righteous shall live till they beget thousands of children" (10:17).

Many Jews also looked forward to bearing children after the grave, such as Rabbi Saadia, who declared that as the living "ate and drank and doubtless married wives, so shall it be after the Resurrection" (in J.R. Dummelow, The One Volume Bible Commentary, N.Y., 1968, 698).

Maimonides in the Middle Ages likewise claimed that "men after the Resurrection will use meat and drink and will beget children" (in ibid.).

Nor do such statements conflict with Christ's saying in Matthew that "in the Resurrection they neither marry nor are given in marriage, but are as the angels" (22:30), for one has to become a "son of the Bridal Chamber" in this world, if he is to be one in the next (Gospel of Philip, Saying 127), This obviously was the understanding of the disciples, who asked which husband a wife would possess in the next world, if she had been married to more than one (Matt, 22:28).

The answer of the Jewish rabbis was usually, "to the first", for that one alone was legitimately and permanently wedded to her. This agrees with Christ's teaching in Matt, 19 that second marriages are generally adulterous, since the first one is enduring and cannot be broken by mortal means (vs., 6, 9).

Furthermore, the Valentinians pointed out that "as the angels" really meant married, for the "angels" (Matt. 18:10) are the pre-existent counterparts of men's souls, which are reunited with them after death (R. M. Grant, "The Mystery of Marriage in the Gospel of Philip", 132).

Christ's belief in the permanency of marriage was reemphasized by his enigmatic reference to the "eunuch" in Matt. 19:12. A careful reading of vss. 9-12 shows that the "eunuch" is one who complies with the Savior's hard doctrine enjoining strict fidelity to one's spouse, even in face of separation. In other words, the husband who has lost a wife is required to forego remarriage "for the kingdom of heaven's sake", for the original union is lasting and unbreakable, Clement of Alexandria actually uses this explanation in the Miscellanies (3. 6:50), saying that the so-called "eunuch" is one who remains continent after the loss of a spouse, for in the eyes of the Church, the couple is still united.

Quentin Quesnell has recently developed this ideal of the "eunuch" in an illuminating article which shows very convincingly that the term did not originally imply celibacy, but one's continuing devotion to a lost loved one. Indeed, it specifically demonstrates a "determination to express that fidelity forever...a step toward inaugurating a world where all men will love perfectly and fully" (italics added; "Made Themselves Eunuchs for the Kingdom of Heaven", Catholic Bible Quarterly 30, 1968,

50

358).

The ideal of continence after enforced separation seems to lie behind Paul's notion of the agamos, as well, an expression which is shown by 1 Cor. 7:11 to refer specifically to those who have lost their companion, not to those who never married.

"Let not the wife depart from her husband; but even if she departs, let her remain agamos, or be reconciled to her husband."

This must have been Paul's own state, for he urges that the "agamois" (pl.) and widows...remain even as I", though if they cannot, he allows them the right to marry again, for "it is better to marry than to burn (with lust)" (vss. 8-9).

This state of agamos, moreover, is clearly contrasted with parthenos, "virgin", in vs. 25. Indeed, Paul claimed that he had no commandment from the Lord respecting "virginity" (vs. 25).

Modern scholars now recognize that Paul's supposed "antipathy" towards marriage has only been read into his writings by faulty translations or misunderstanding. The "advice" respecting celibacy at the beginning of 1 Cor. 7, for example, is really a repetition of the correspondent's question: "With reference to the matter about which you wrote: is it good for a man to have sexual relations with a woman?" (trans. by Wm. Orr and James Walther, Anchor Bible, 1 Corinthians, N.Y.. 1976, 265).

The answer, of course, was "Let every man have his own wife, and let every woman have her own husband" (vs. 2).

Paul's hesitation to recommend marriage to the Corinthians "in view of the world passing away" (vs. 31), most likely reflects his conciliatory attitude towards certain converts who were involved in a local "ascetic trend" (Orr and Walther, op. cit., 224), as well as the personal care of one who had recently suffered the loss of his own spouse (cf. Eusebius, History III. 30).

In any case, it is well-known that those who lived closest to the Savior were married. The early apostles and disciples were men who complied with the Wedded Image in the Temple. As such, they were indeed "sons of the Bridal Chamber".

Clement of Alexandria unequivocally taught that all should marry as the apostles did (Who is the Real Man that Shall Be Saved? 14, 22, 27), Eusebius (History III.30) lists Peter, Philip and Paul among "the apostles that lived in marriage". Clement also understood Paul's words in 1 Cor. 9:5 to mean that the apostles travelled about with wives; Acts 1:12-14 records that all were present with their wives and children in the Upper Room after the Resurrection. The Epistles generally indicate that marriage was expected of bishops, elders, deacons and the like (1 Tim. 3:2, 5; 5:14; Tit. 1:6; Rom. 16:3; 1 Cor. 7:2; etc.). In fact, about forty of the early Popes were married (John A. O'Brian, "Why Priests Marry", The Christian Century 87: 417), (See also Wm. Phipps, Was Jesus Married? N.Y., 1970, 99ff).

When Danielou shows that the Gnostics received their doctrine of Christ's nuptials with Sophia from the Church (Theology of Jewish Christianity, 301-11), we must therefore suppose that they also received the concomitant doctrine of human marriage

separation — Reunion
individual / Fall & Redemption

Moses

from the same source. There is little reason, then, to believe that the Gnostic "Bridal Chamber" was anything but an elaboration of authentic Jewish and Christian practice, begun in the Temple.

In our own A Great Mystery, we have been able to show that this essential connection between divine and human marriages ran like a leit-motif through the entire history of Jewish and Christian thought. Since God is "male and female" together (Gen, 1:27), the Perfect Man must also be male and female united (vs. 28). Death came into the world with the Perfect Man's initial separation (Gen. 2:21), which could only be repaired when male and female again become One (vs. 24). This, according to the latest evidence, was the general teaching of the Primitive Church.

The imitation of divine sexual union can be documented for several millennia, beginning with the Semitic hieros games cult.

The Sumerian reenactment of the Sacred Marriage of Dumuzi and Inanna, for example, continued in the Babylonian cult of Tammuz and Ishtar for at least two thousand years (S.N. Kramer, The Sacred Marriage Rite, Indiana University Press, 1969, 49). A similar cult involving the Canaanite Baal and Anath was paralleled by the Israelite worship of Yahweh and "Asherah-Ashtoreth"--complete with sacred prostitutes and general sexual license (Deut. 16121; Judg. 6:25; 1 Kings 21:7; Jer. 7:18; 44:17-19, 25; etc.)--a practice retrospectively condemned as "whoredom" and "whoring after other gods" (Ex. 34:15-17; Lev. 17:7; Num. 15:31; Deut. 31:16= etc.). The book of Hosea is an account of the reformer's attempt to substitute an allegorized "marriage" between Yahweh and Israel for this literal hieros gamos. Thus, the category of "heavenly unions" was enlarged to include the covenant "marriage" of God and his People (=Christ and the Church).

These "heavenly unions" were always imitated by various forms of human sexuality, such as cult prostitution (1 Sam. 2:22; Hos. 4:13-14; Jer. 3:2; Ezek. 23:40-41; etc.), legitimate married union (Gen. 1:27-28; Hos. 1:2-3; Eph. 570:32; Tos. Yebamoth 8:4; Zohar III:7a; 296a; etc. Gnostic libertinism (Epiphanius, Panarion 26.8:2-3; Clement, Miscellanies 3.8:2; Irenaeus, Against Heresies 1.6:4; etc.), and even sexless unions with so-called virgines subintroductae, who symbolized the Church (Shepherd of Hermas 5.10:3; Acts of Thomas 6ff; etc.). Thus, the essential correspondence between heavenly and earthly unions continued even after celibacy began to erode the Church's doctrine of normal marriage.

In each of these stages of hierogamy, human marriage served as a "symbolic reference" to the divine. Of particular interest was the tradition in which a prophet's marriage to a fallen woman was chosen to symbolize Yahweh's union with "adulterous" Israel. The earliest known example of this was Hosea's marriage to the prostitute Comer, which became the human symbol of the Lord's "marriage" to his wayward people (Hos. 1:2). In both cases, the "husband's" love was intended to selflessly redeem the weaker partner (cf. also 5:25-27).

Another prophet who redeemed a "fallen woman" was Simon Magus (Acts 8:9-14). In this case, Simon himself claimed to be the redeemer of his people. According to Irenaeus, he foretold how he would appear to the Jews as the Son, to the Samaritans as

52

the Father, and to others as the Holy Spirit. His symbolic wife was a prostitute named Helen, whom he had rescued from a brothel at Tyre, and who represented the "lost Sheep" he came to save. Scholars have recognized important parallels between Helen and the Semitic Goddess, for she was traditionally Patroness of Lust., as well as the archetype of God's pre-existent "Wisdom" or "Israel" (R.M. Grant, Gnosticism and Early Christianity, 1st ed., 85). (See also Gershom Scholem, "Zur Entwicklungsgeschichte der kabbalistischen Konzeption der Schechinah", Eranos Jahrbuch 21, 1952, 51, who shows that the Goddess became known in rabbinical circles as the kenesseth Ysrael, the "Community of Israel", showing once again that man has a divine origin, being derived from a Heavenly Mother, or God's feminine nature.)

Even more striking, though, are the parallels between Simon and Jesus. Both were redeemers of their people; and it can hardly be coincidence that the Gospel of Philip also makes Jesus the husband of a woman traditionally thought to have been an adulteress-- Mary Magdelene! (Sayings 31, 55).

Whether or not Jesus was actually married to this woman, or if she was really a prostitute, is impossible for us to say. What is important is that Christians readily recognized a tradition equating the Redeemer and his "fallen woman" with Yahweh-Israel, Hosea-Gomer and Simon-Helen, as did even Paul, when he declared in Ephesians that a man's love for his wife should be the same sort of sacrificial love shown by Christ for an unworthy Church.

Other Apocrypha also frequently make Jesus and Mary intimate partners. The Gospel of Mary, for example, says: "We know that the Savior loved (Mary) more than other women (Papyrus Berolinensis 10).

In the Pistis Sophia she receives virtually all of the attention, even to the slighting of the male apostles, and is promised a heavenly throne above their own (ch. 96). The Gospel of Peter says that Mary Magdalene came to the tomb on Resurrection morning to do "what women customarily did for their beloved departed" (50), This may well explain why even in the NT she was the first person to whom the Risen Lord revealed himself (Mk. 16:9-11; John 20:14-18).

She again figures prominently in the Gospel of Thomas, where Jesus proclaims his intent to make her male (Logion 114). This expression commonly meant in the literature of Judaism and the early Church to be sexually complete, i.e. "One Flesh": "When you make the two one, you shall become sons of Man" (Logion 106). For "if he is One, he will be filled with light, but if he is Divided, he will be filled with darkness" (Logion 61).

Here we encounter again the theme of sexual unity, described in the Gospel of Philip and the Zohar, where marriage is a re-creation of the Divine Image of male and female in perfect union, whereas "femaleness" meant divided sexuality (Baer. op. cit., 49-50).

It was widely held, therefore, that salvation would come only when the "females" became "males", or "when the two shall be one, and the outside as the inside, and the male with the female neither male nor female" (2 Clement 12).

This "neutralized" state of oneness--though applicable both to the marriage of

53

Christ and the Church and to man and wife--curiously recalls the "eunuch" whom Christ referred to in Matt. 12. Indeed, 2 Clement goes on to describe a man and woman who have become so close as to cancel all extraneous sexual lust for outsiders: "By the male with the female, neither male nor female, he meaneth this: that a brother seeing a sister shall have no thought of her as a female, and a sister seeing a brother shall have no thought of him as a male".

The Gospel of Philip employs the same concept of sexual oneness to explain how a man and wife are able to rise past the hostile "powers" into heaven:

> Among the unclean spirits there are male and female. The male are they which unite with the souls which inhabit a female form; but the female are they which are mingled with those in a male form...None shall be able to escape them, since they detain him, if he does not receive a male power or a female, which is the bridegroom or the bride (Saying 61).

Both Wilson and Till (as noted above) take this passage to refer to a literal marriage (Wilson, op. cit., 121-2; of. also 184), as the text itself suggests:

> When the ignorant women see a male sitting alone, they leap down upon him and sport with him and defile him. So also the ignorant men, when they see a beautiful woman sitting alone...But if they see the man and his wife sitting beside one another, the female cannot come in to the man, nor the male come in to the woman (Saying 61, cont.)

This same thought apparently lies behind Paul's two statements in Corinthians: "Better to marry than to burn (with lust)" (1 Cor. 7:9), and "Let the woman cover her head...because of the angels" (11:6, 107, for unattached "halves" are always subject to illegitimate enticements (cf. Gen. 6:2-4).

The rest of Saying 61 adds that the soul and its pre-existent counterpart are united at the same time in the Bridal Chamber, prefigured by the "mirror-image" of the earthly union. Thus, "resurrection" was guaranteed to the married partners.

It should now be clear that the texts from Nag Hammadi are nothing more than late expressions of tendencies natural to Judeo-Christian religion from the very start. Even as decadent survivals, however, they provide invaluable evidence of the cultural roots which produced them, It is now obvious that the Gnostics did not invent their ubiquitous image of sexual union, nor did they employ it merely to represent the sexless union of "Christ-Holy Spirit" and "Mankind", as Ms. Layton erroneously supposes. Rather did they adopt a traditional and venerated symbol reflecting both the immemorial sanctity of marriage and God's union with Man, just as it did at the dawn of Semitic prehistory, when man's procreative power was equated with the creative power of God which he bore. Even after the heresy of celibacy attempted to "spiritualize" this ancient doctrine, its original literalness was still plainly visible in the notorious cult-icons, i.e. the embracing Cherubim in the Jerusalem Temple.

A good case in point is the 3rd century "Bridal Chamber" scene in Questions of Mary, recorded by Epiphanius in the Panarion. There, Jesus is shown having carnal intercourse with Mary Magdalene, saying, "We must so do in order to have eternal life".

But by the 3rd century, the author had made Jesus to practice a revolting form of "birth control", with the intent of thwarting the imprisonment of souls in bodies. Nevertheless, in spite of this attempt to "spiritualize" sexual relations, the episode clearly shows what the original object of the rite must have been, i.e. normal marriage, though now degraded into an utter parody of itself.

We should always bear this lesson in mind when we contemplate the Nag Hammadi texts, for Gnosticism ended up as a parody of its own sources. But even parody can be instructive, if we are careful to trace the connecting links which tie it to its origins. And when this is done, the early stages of Gnosticism are always seen to be "incomparably closer" to the initial truth than was heretofore suspected.

R.A. Batey concluded recently that there was once a "widespread nuptial myth", common to early Christianity, Judaism and the Mystery religions, serving as the "central core" around which Gnostic accretions later gathered ("Jewish Gnosticism and the 'Hieros Gamos' of Eph. V:21-33", New Testament Studies 16, 1963-4, 121-7).

J. Paul Sampley also recognized that Paul's language in Eph. 5 and 2 Cor. 11:2 offers "a glimpse into a popular speculation that may have been much more pervasive than the extant early Christian literature indicates" (For the Two Shall Become One Flesh, Cambridge, 1971, 87).

Patai's rediscovery of the embracing Cherubim in the Temple now enables us to see for the first time what that "nuptial myth" was really like, The Nag Hammadi texts further supply some of the lost details of this "Great Mystery" in the Holy of Holies, and remind us of the former importance of that secret Image of God, which men diminish when they refuse to marry.

For Mormons, the importance of these amazing discoveries is obvious.

XI

Why was this "Great Mystery" lost to the world?

Simply because it was taught in secret.

Orthodoxy has long denied that Jews or Christians ever taught in secret, citing as evidence Jesus' words in <u>Matthew</u>, "What ye hear in the ear, that preach ye - upon the housetops" (10:27).

Actually, this is no different than his great missionary commandment: "Go ye therefore and teach all nations...teaching them to observe all things whatsoever I have commanded you" (28:19-20). The disciples, in short, are to freely share the good news of the Gospel (2 Cor. 11:7), holding back nothing from them that earnestly seek after it (<u>Matt</u>. 7,2).

Nevertheless, Jesus cautioned that the "mysteries" were not to be babbled indiscriminately before the unworthy: "Give not that which is holy unto the dogs, neither cast ye your pearls before swine, lest they trample them under their feet and turn again and rend you" (7:6). Even his admonition in 10:27 is prefaced with the implicit understanding that some things were reserved for private instruction ("What I tell you in darkness..."). Thus, the disciples were always to use discretion when engaged in proselyting.

But regardless of argument, the facts are that both Jews and Christians <u>did</u> teach in secret. Even the NT shows that Jesus taught things to which only the Inner Circle of disciples was privy to: "Unto you is given to know the mystery of the kingdom of God; but unto them that are without, all these things are done in parables, that seeing they may see and not perceive, and hearing may hear and not understand" (<u>Mk</u>. 4:11-12).

Objective scholarship has long recognized the discreet nature of Jesus' teaching throughout the Gospels, "as if Jesus, like a hierophant led the twelve and those around him 'step by step' into the mysteries of the 'Church." (Schille, Form<u>geschichte</u> 18; in Morton Smith, <u>Clement of Alexandria and the Secret Gospel of Mark</u>, Cambridge, Mass., 1973, 200). Even his defensive words at the Trial ("In secret have I said nothing"; <u>John</u> 18:20) necessarily reflect a charge of secret teaching, a charge which is curiously supported by his own words in 16:25: "These things have I spoken to you in proverbs, but the time cometh when I shall no more speak to you in proverbs, but I shall show you plainly of the Father".

That time <u>did</u> come, during the secret post-Resurrection teaching (<u>Lk</u>. 24:25f; <u>Acts</u> 1:3). At that time, the disciples (who previously comprehended little, though they had heard everything contained in the canonical Gospels!) were finally made to understand the Savior's mission with sufficient clarity that they immediately embarked on the most amazing missionary activity ever recorded!

This secret "40-day teaching" became the stock-in-trade of Gnostic writings, which strove always to piece together the secrets of the early Church. Many of the Nag Hammadi texts begin with the claim that "these are the secret words which Jesus spoke during the 40 days after the Resurrection". Several alternate numbers are also used, showing that they did not slavishly copy one another, but were reporting a genuine tradition which everyone recognized.

Paul also claimed to "speak the Wisdom of God in a mystery" (1 Cor. 2:7), recalling at one time how he himself had learned marvelous things "which it is not lawful for men to utter" (2 Cor. 12:4). Morton Smith has now demonstrated beyond question that the term "mystery" was commonly used in the NT to mean either "secret instruction" or "secret rite" (op. cit., 178-208). Nor does the fact that such secrets were to be revealed by the Spirit after Christ's Resurrection mean that they became known to everyone, for present-day "orthodoxy" possesses absolutely nothing but what is contained in the public teaching of the canon.

(Significantly, Latter Day Saints still maintain that the real "secret' instruction of the Temple is given only by revelation to those who attend with the proper desire; see John A. Widtsoe, "Temple Worship", Utah Genealogical and Historical Magazine, Apr. 1921, 63,)

"In sum, the Gospels all represent Jesus as teaching in secret; Paul certainly had secret doctrines and Lk. and Jn, presuppose them. When Christianity first appears in the writings of Pagan authors it is described as a secret society (Pliny, Epistolae ad Traianum 96.7)" (Smith, op. hit., 201).

Judaism was also a "mystery religion" in the full Graeco-Roman sense of the word (ibid., 181), being compared by Plutarch to the Eleusinian mysteries (Quaestiones Conviviales 4:6). Apocalyptic Judaism from the very beginning was the repository of secret doctrine that was previously handed down through a lengthy period of oral transmission. Even after it was committed to writing, it was never circulated among the masses. By the close of the intertestamental period, the writer of 4 Ezra could refer to no less than seventy secret books which were exclusively limited to the use of the "wise" (14:46), books which became especially venerated by the Primitive Church, gaining equal footing with the canonical Scriptures (vss. 45-6).

"Reference in the Church Fathers and in later rabbinic writings confirms this widespread influence of apocalyptic and suggests that those apocalyptic books now extant are only a fraction of what must have been at one time a very considerable literature" (D.S. Russell, The Method and Message of Jewish Apocalyptic, 29). "Those which survive no doubt represent the books which were most highly valued among the Christians" (italics added; ibid., 34). It is to this important body of literature that the presently available Apocrypha--the last of which were the Nag Hammadi texts --belong.

As indicated earlier, the secret origin and immortality of the soul were among the chief esoteric doctrines of apocalyptic.

The literature of Qumran also belonged to apocalyptic, and contains frequent reference to secret doctrines which are not to be disclosed to outsiders. The Community Rule, for instance, speaks of "those things hidden from Israel" which the founder of the sect received for restricted use in the Community (1QS 8:11). Every member of this esoteric group was commanded to "conceal the teaching of the Law from men of falsehood (outsiders), but shall impart true knowledge and righteous judgment to those who have chosen the way...and shall thus instruct them in the mysteries of marvelous truth" (9:17-18).

God revealed these mysteries solely to the sectaries at Qumran (1QH 1:21). Thus, secret knowledge was part and parcel of Qumran belief, and represented the same mentality which characterized early converts to the Church. R. E. Brown has also shown in great detail that the NT word "mystery" exactly parallels that of the Dead Sea Scrolls and other apocryphal literature (The Semitic Background of the Term 'Mystery' in the New Testament, Philadelphia, 1968).

Pharisaic Judaism was likewise full of esoteric doctrines (Smith, op. cit., 181-3). It is well-known that the Tetragrammaton, YHWH, was uttered only in secret in the Temple, for which reason it's very pronunciation was lost after the destruction of Jerusalem in 70 A.D. Secret knowledge about the Throne and Body of God--including the "Limbs of the Lover"--was taught in rabbinic Judaism at least as early as the 2nd century, using Song of Songs and Ezekiel as its chief texts (Gershom Scholem Jewish Gnosticism, Merkabah Mysticism and Talmudic Tradition, N.Y. 1960, 38-39). Only a select few, who had reached "full maturity", were permitted to enter into this esoteric study, which went under the name of Shiur Komah, the mystical "Body of God". It was also about this time--after 70 A.D. and the loss of the Temple--that writers such as Rabbi Akiba began to specifically mention Song of Songs in relation to the mystery of the Cherubim (see quotation, above).

The Mishna also forbade open discussion of the mysteries of the heavens, the underworld, the pre-existence, and the eschaton ("what is above? what is beneath? what was before time? and what will be hereafter?" Chagiga 2:1). Such secret doctrines could only be taught to those past the age of thirty, and only in groups of two or three.

That the Church continued this tradition is shown by numerous statements in the early literature, e.g. the Clementine Recognitions, which says, "I could tell you both whence souls are, and where and how they were made; only it is not permitted to describe these things to you (2:6), and Origen, who referred to the doctrine of the "entrance of souls into bodies" as the "secret of a King", which should be "kept close" from outsiders (quotation above).

Morton Smith believes that baptism was first given as a secret rite (Mk. 14: 51-2), though as the Church grew, and it became a common experience, "it declined in prestige and there was a corresponding growth of secret teachings which professed to reveal something more" (op. cit., 183-4). While we may not necessarily agree with the original secrecy of baptism, the secret "something more" has been abundantly demonstrated by now.

There is a certain amount of logic, however, in keeping baptism a secret rite, for the most important question about the "mystery of the kingdom" (Mk. 4:11) would have been how to get in, and it is well-known that baptism was viewed as a symbol of the initiate's becoming "One Flesh" with Christ (1 Cor. 12:13). But, thanks to the vistas opened up by Patai's recent rediscovery of the secret Cherubim, we now know that not merely baptism, but the whole complex of ideas associated with the "marriage" in the Bridal Chamber, was the real "mystery of the kingdom", which the neophyte experienced by "marriage" to Christ <u>Rom</u>. 7:41 <u>2 Cor</u>. 11:2).

An important aspect of this "marriage" was the doctrine of Christ's pre-existent espousal to the Church. We have already seen that the pre-existent Church appears in the <u>Shepherd of Hermas</u> and elsewhere as "six young men" and the Lord, It has recently been shown by Danielou that the circle of the apostles secretly interpreted the six days of Creation (the <u>hexaemera)</u> as an allegory on the creation of these six "archangels" (<u>Theology of Jewish Christianity,</u> 108, 166-72, 299ff). Christ, being the "seventh", or chief, "archangel", corresponded to the seventh day, or "Day of Rest" (Clement, <u>Miscellanies</u> VI,138:1).

The <u>hexaemera,</u> in short, represented an esoteric account of the <u>spiritual</u> Creation, which preceded the physical Creation.

But after the "Lord's Day"--the beginning of the following week--replaced the Jewish Sabbath as the Holy Day of the Church, writers began to associate it with an eighth, or transcendent, Being, who was not an "angel", but the <u>Progenitor</u> of an-gels, the Unknown God, Thus, the Nag Hammadi texts frequently speak of seven lower spheres(the "Hebdomad"), over which there reigns the transcendent sphere of the Unknown Father (the "Ogdoad"), all derived by extension from the secret "Hexameron" speculation of the Primitive Church.

But the esoteric interpretation of <u>Genesis</u> did not end there, The creation of man and woman after the "image of God" was also taken as a spiritual history of the "Perfect Man", i.e. "a pre-existent celestial Adam distinct from the earthly one who sinned" (Danielou, <u>op. cit</u>., 309-10). It was this "archetypal humanity" that was destroyed when Adam and Eve were separated (<u>Gen</u>. 2:21), and was re-created when they "clave together" again as "One Flesh" (vs. 24). Thus, the account in <u>Genesis</u> 1-2 is both the <u>exoteric</u> story of man's earthly creation, and the <u>esoteric</u> story of his pre-existent counterpart.

This secret doctrine of man's descent out of the heavens continued to be the subject of speculation in the Nag Hammadi texts, which generally contain two complementary accounts of the matters 1-The name of the High God is "Man", after whom the race of man is named; 2-"Man" is a divine ancestor of earthly man, also called "Anthropos", "Adamas", "Primal Man", etc., to emphasize his archetypal humanity.

These theories are actually aspects of a single belief. In the first, man is described <u>theomorphically,</u> i.e. in the image of God. In the second, God is described <u>anthropomor-phically,</u> i.e. after the image of man. In either case, Man and God are of the same species.

That God was already called "Man", even at the time of the Savior, has been suggested by M. Ford ("The Son of Man'--A Euphemism?", JBL 87, 257-66), and Edwin Freed ("The Son of Man and the Fourth Gospel", <u>JBL</u> 86, 1-9), who convincingly demonstrate that "Man" was understood by the Jews who crucified Christ as a special name for God, and "Son of Man" as a name for his Son. To use the name "Son of Man" for oneself, then, would have been viewed as blasphemy, or "making oneself equal to God".

This was also one of Joseph Smith's distinctive teachings--found in no other

Son of Man = God

Perfect Man =
Man of Holiness

contemporary writings; for in the <u>Book of Moses,</u> it is clearly stated that God's secret name is "Man of Holiness", and his Son's, "<u>Son of Man</u>" (6:57), Since a common variant of "Man" in the Nag Hammadi texts was ("Perfect Man") this is an exact equivalent, for "holy" simply means "whole" or "perfect" in a moral sense. "<u>Man</u> of Holiness", in other words, is a perfect translation for "Perfect Man" (see H.- M. Schenke, <u>Per Gott</u> "<u>Mensch</u>" in der <u>Gnosis, Gottingen,</u> 1962, 6-15).

To summarize, there can never again be any doubt that both Israel and the Church taught certain things in secret. The "Great Mystery" in the Bridal Chamber, especially, was the grand secret <u>par excellence</u>--as our total ignorance of the matter these nineteen hundred years so strikingly demonstrates.

Everything associated with becoming "sons of the Bridal Chamber" was part of this esoteric knowledge, including the secret origin and immortality of the soul, the entrance of souls into bodies (dual paternity), the necessity of human marriage, and the espousal of the pre-existent Church to Christ.

The Bridal Chamber always remained a secret from the rest of the world. Even its Jewish antecedents had traditionally been treated as a secret cult. Philo thus spoke of the mystery in the Holy of Holies as if it were a "commonplace to his readers" (Goodenough, <u>By Light, Light:</u> 23). This shows that its esoteric nature was well-recognized in Israel.

Rendel Harris also quotes a passage belonging to Philo, which says; "It is not permitted to speak of the sacred Mysteries to the uninitiated until they shall have been purified with the proper purification...To declare the Mysteries to the uninitiated would mean the destruction of the laws of the most sacred Mystery" (<u>Fragments</u> of <u>Philo</u> <u>Judaeus,</u> Cambridge, 1886, 69).

These and similar passages analyzed by Goodenough led him to conclude that the Jews had a "true Mystery" of <u>their own</u>, in contrast to the false mysteries of Paganism, in which <u>secret objects</u> "manifest to the sight" were shown to the initiates (<u>op. cit.</u>, 262), As we have abundantly seen, these true mysteries were long continued by the Primitive Christians and Gnostics.

As for the <u>secret objects</u> "manifest to the sight", these can only have been the embracing Cherubim in the Holy of Holies, which Josephus once said were "unlawful" to reveal to outsiders.

-XII-

What difference do such "secret doctrines" make? Did not the Savior promise resurrection to all who believed on his name?

The Nag Hammadi texts distinguish between three levels of spiritual attainment after deaths the hylics, or "materialists", the psychics, equivalent to the Israelites and ordinary Christians; and the pneumatics, or "spirituals", who reach full expression of their divine potential. One of the new texts correspondingly bears the title, Treatise on the Three Natures.

This has long been a doctrine of Mormonism, though one which "orthodoxy" hotly denies. Today it is agreed by all scholars that the Primitive Church recognized and taught such a doctrine.

Although Gnostic texts also refer to "seven" heavens, these are nothing but an elaboration of the original three, for the seven "cosmic spheres" (probably of Meso-potamian origin) are simply divisions within the second heaven (Danielou, Theology of Jewish Christianity, 176fn), Judaism also traditionally recognized three heavens, characterized by various astral bodies appropriate to their degree of splendor (cf. 1 Cor. 15:41; Danielou, ibid., 174).

That the early Church taught of these three "degrees of glory" in the heavens is shown by Christ's reference in Matt. 13 to the Good Seed, which produces fruit, "some a hundred fold, some sixty fold, some thirty fold" (vs. 8). Evidence of this interpretation is contained in many extant writings which explicitly describe man's heavenly future in these same terms (e.g. Pseudo Cyprian's Of the Hundredfold, Sixty-fold and the Thirtyfold).

The earliest Church Fathers also taught that there would be "three degrees of glory" in the next world. Papias, for example, said that "those who are worthy of an abode in heaven shall go there; others shall enjoy the delights of Paradise, and others shall possess the splendor of the city" (Relics of the Elders 5).

Furthermore, he specifically relates these future abodes to the "hundredfold, sixtyfold and thirtyfold", for "in my Father's house are many mansions", and a share is given to all "as each one is or shall be worthy" (ibid.).

Irenaeus repeated the same doctrine, claiming that it was a genuine teaching of the Elders, i.e. the Apostles (Against Heresies V. 36:1). This doctrine of three heavens is also found in the Testament of Levi (3:1-4), one of the books quoted by the Savior in the Sermon on the Mount.

That the Nag Hammadi texts spoke of different levels above, then, is simply a continuation of authentic, Judeo-Christian belief, Only those who were "sons of the Bridal Chamber" were destined for the highest position in the heavenly worlds, for only those who enter into the earthly Bridal Chamber will enter into the Pleroma, or highest heaven, with the Savior.

The lot of those who attained to this highest level of immortality was described in many of the early texts as deification, in contrast to the "orthodox" notion of mere

61

sanctification. The Latter Day Saint definition of a "god" is one whose glory is "a fulness and a continuation of the seeds forever" (Doctrine and Covenants 132:19). This is the exact same promise made to the righteous in 1 Enoch 10:17 that they would continue to beget "thousands" after the Resurrection (see above). The same text says that these righteous individuals will be transformed into the likeness of the Messiah (90:38), Thus, Enoch, the "hero" of this work is greeted with these words as he arrives in heaven: "Thou are the Son of Man who art born unto righteousness, and righteousness abides over thee, and the righteousness of the Head of Days foresakes thee not" (70:14).

If the meaning of this seems obscure to modern readers, it is reemphasized in other Enoch texts. In 2 Enoch, for example, the Patriarch is clothed with celestial garments and transformed into the likeness of God's "angels" (the LXX's translation for "sons of God" in Deut. 32:8). But in 3 Enoch, the old Sage is introduced by the name of "Metatron", a Jewish term for the Anthropos (a variant of the Redeemed Redeemer in Christian texts). He is given a throne only slightly lower than God's, is put in charge of all the treasures of heaven, and is described as a "lesser Yahweh"! (12:5).

E, Sjoberg explains that these texts describe not merely the translation of someone into heaven "who had already been the Son of Man during his earthly life, but rather the *exaltation of a man*, like other men, who became the Son of Man at his translation" (italics added; Der Menschensohn im Athiopischen Henochbuch, Lund, 1946, 168ff).

The Talmud also records the belief that "if the righteous desired it, they could by living a life of absolute purity be creators...But for their iniquities, their power could equal God's, and they could create a world" (Sanhedrin 65b). Those who taught this doctrine were probably the same Jews who were commanded in the 2nd century to abandon their literal understanding of the expression "sons of God", and with it, the natural corollary that "he whose root is divine" possesses divine potential (see above).

Christians about the same time were teaching that the pre-existent souls were destined from before the world to participate in God's work, "to increase and to build it, and to be masters of Creation" (Shepherd of Hermas V.3:4). Hippolytus likewise records the belief that "if another had equally fulfilled the demands of the Law, he would also have become Christ, because through the same deeds others can also become Christs" (quoted by H. J. Schoeps, Theologie und Geschichte des Judenchristentums, Tubingen, 1949, 53). Even Jews as late as the Middle Ages continued to teach that the purified souls would enter the highest heaven to be deified and given creative work, not merely to be passively reunited with God (Leo Schaya, The Universal Meaning of the Kabbalah, London, 1971, 80, 167).

It was no deviation from normal traditions, then, for the Nag Hammadi texts to teach that the one who becomes a "son of the Bridal Chamber" will no longer be a mere Christian, but a Christ (Gospel of Philip, Saying 67): "You saw the Spirit, you became spirit. You saw Christ, you became a Christ. You saw the Father, you shall become a Father...You see yourself, and what you see you shall become" (Saying 44).

This is because in each man there "dwells an infinite power...the root of the universe" (Simon Magus, in Hippolytus, Refutations 6:9), This power exists "in a latent condition in everyone" (ibid., 6:17), To help us realize this potential is the aim of our

Father. "A horse begets a horse, a man begets a man, a god begets a god; so it is with the bridegroom and the bride. Their children (= "sons of God") originate from the Bridal Chamber" (Gospel of Philip, Saying 102).

This, according to the Nag Hammadi texts, is the true meaning of rebirth after the Divine Image in the Bridal Chamber (Saying 67), or the restoration of the divine nature we brought with us from our Heavenly Home.

Having discussed the main doctrinal issues common to Primitive Christianity, early Judaism, the Nag Hammadi texts and Mormonism, it is desirable that we attempt to broadly summarize the resulting picture.

Indeed, in many respects it is a single picture, or "one big book", as the Mormon scholar, Hugh Nibley, has called it (Since Cumorah, Salt Lake City, 1967, 89-95). One early investigator, William H. Brownlee, thus noted from the very first how the texts from Qumran, the Damascus Covenanters, the Egyptian Therapeutae, John the Baptist's movement, and Primitive Christianity all exhibited "striking affinities" with one another (Biblical Archaeologist, Sept, 1960, 50), And Frank M. Cross, Jr., drawing on the amazing parallels between Qumran and the Church, dubbed the former the "Church of Anticipation", since it looked forward in so many prophetic ways to Christianity (The Ancient Library of Qumran and Modern Biblical Studies, N.Y., 1968, 181-4). Most scholars today concede without hesitation that the same kind of thought which characterized the sectaries at Qumran also penetrated deeply into the Johannine corpus of the NT, and to a lesser but significant degree, the Synoptics, and the writings of Paul.

Doubtlessly, there were important differences, too. No one--least of all the Mormons--would claim that the Savior brought nothing new to those Jews who anxiously awaited him. But there can be no doubt that the newly discovered kinds of Judaism became the main "seed bed of the New Testament" (Caster, The Dead Sea Scriptures, 1956 ed., 12), or the "preparation for the Gospel", as Eusebius anciently described it. Thus God works in history, making ready the soil in which to plant his word. For this reason, the similarities are far more important than the differences, especially when a historical connection can be shown between them.

The apocalyptic milieu especially--with its secret revelations concerning the last days, pre-existence, the coming of the Son of Man, the dualism, the doctrine of the transcendent Kingdom--became the property of the first Christians, and the chief source of their theological nourishment. For a time, apocalyptic Judaism and Christianity were virtually identical; it is in fact difficult to tell which group first wrote certain parts of the apocalyptic texts, so closely were they shared, and so interchangeable was their employment. Their doctrines thus appear to have been cut from the same cloth, and to reflect the same inspired longing for eternal realities.

"To affirm that the Jews in Christ's time did not believe in pre-existence, is simply inaccurate", wrote a scholar nearly eighty years ago (A Dictionary of the Bible, ed. Hastings, N.Y., 1903, IV:63). But we now know that it would be just as inaccurate to suppose that the early Christians did not share this "commonplace of apocalyptic" (Hamerton-Kelly, op. cit., 9).

The same commonality of belief is also true of the other apocalyptic ideas, including angelology, spiritual communion with the heavens, revelation, prophecy, and control of the powers which impede man's progress through the worlds.

"Might I not write to you things full of mystery?" hinted Ignatius, in the 2nd century. "For even I...am able to understand heavenly things, the angelic orders, the different sets of angels and hosts, the distinctions between powers and dominions, the mightiness of the Aeons, and the pre-eminence of the Cherubim and Seraphim, the sublimity of the Spirit, the kingdom of the Lord, and above all, the incomparable majesty of almighty God" (To the Trallians V), "But I fear to do so", he added, "lest I should inflict injury on you who are but babes in Christ."

Thus spoke the authentic voice of apocalyptic, while it yet flourished in its original splendor, guarding its secrets from those who were not yet prepared to receive them.

But soon after, "there came a parting of the ways...Apocalyptic was abandoned by normative Judaism and became the (sole) property of the Christian Church" (Russell, op. cit., 85). Until the ascendency of philosophy and metaphysics at Rome, the Church remained custodian of the Semitic thought-forms inherited from the past. She it was who for a few fading years continued to teach the survival of the soul after death and its return to God, to be clothed in resurrected flesh, that it might continue its creative work throughout eternity (Shepherd of Hermas).

With the spread of the Gospel into the Latin world, however, even the remaining Semitic character of the Church was eventually lost, Just as the Savior had fore-told, his followers were torn with heresy and dissention (Matt. 13:25; 24:5, 24; cf. also Acts 20:29; 1 Cor. 11:18; Gal. 1:6; 1 Tim. 1:6; 4:1: 2 Tim. 1:15; 3:5; 4:4; Tit. 1:161 James 4:1; etc.). Indeed, it had been prophesied that the Savior would not return to earth until after a general apostasy, "for that day shall not come except there come a falling away first, and the man of sin be revealed" (2 Thess. 2:3). This would be the "night when no man can work" (John 9:4), when "the prince of the world cometh, and hath nothing in me" (14:30), or the so-called "Wintertime of the Just", referred to by early Church writers (cf. Shepherd of Hermas S. 3:4).

Those who clung last to the Church's apocalyptic origins--the Gnostics--began to look down with hatred and scorn on the new "orthodoxy", "who were for them the false believers" (Bauer, op. cit., xxii), for it appears that these ancient manifestations of Christianity which are presently rejected as *heresy* "originally had not been such at all, but were at least here and there the *only forms of the new religion*; that is, for those regions, they were simply Christianity" (italics added; ibid.).

What is certain is that Gnosticism was the last to have employed almost exclusively the original thought forms of Christianity, though even they eventually de-generated into grotesque excesses, and were swept into oblivion by victorious "orthodoxy", with its worldly politics and simple moralizing.

We can see now how very essential the writings of Qumran and other "hetero-dox" Jewish texts are for the proper understanding of Primitive Christianity, as well as the Gnostic writings which brought this ancient chapter of history to a close, Although the Scrolls themselves did "not contain Gnostic ideas...they do belong to the broader movement of apocalyptic Judaism which may well have been a forerunner of Gnosticism" (MacRae, "Gnosticism and New Testament Studies", Bible Today, 1968, 2629).

This conservative opinion is all the more certain today. James M. Robinson even concludes that certain NT writings, particularly the Johannine works, served as the actual conduit between the Scrolls and the Gnostics, "a development from the pre- or proto-Gnosticism of Qumran through intermediate stages attested both in the New Testament and in part of Nag Hammadi into the full gnostic systems of the second century A.D. Thus a gnosticizing trajectory emerges, on which the Gospel of John has its history-of-religions location" (Trajectories, 266).

It is also significant that the man called the "First Gnostic"--Simon Magus--was said by Hippolytus and Eusebius to have been a disciple of John the Baptist, and thus a representative of that same apocalyptic milieu which created Qumran. He it was who is known to have taught one of the earliest versions of man's pre-existent descent from the Father. R. McLain Wilson therefore suggests that a common tradition united Jewish "heterodoxy", as expressed in the Dead Sea Scrolls, Alexandrian Judaism and the "Samaritan gnosis" of Simon, Menander, Dositheus, etc., a tradition which later surfaced in Gnostic Christianity ("Simon, Dositheus and the Dead Sea Scrolls", Zeitschrift für Religions- und Geistesgeschichte, 1957, 21-30).

That the Gnostics themselves finally became "apostates" from the pure Gospel of Christ was perhaps more the result of feeding in isolation upon their own substance than of outside influences. In other words, the Gnostics were speculative theologizers who carried the traditional doctrines to fantastic extremes, exaggerating the significance of isolated Scriptures beyond their original intent.

Their Docetism, for example, was merely the ultimate extension of such ideas as Paul's "spiritual" resurrection-body (1 Cor. 15:44f), Jesus' "Fear not them which kill the body, but are not able to kill the soul" (Matt. 10:28), and John's aletheia (KJV "Truth"), the "divine reality" which is opposed to the world. Similarly, their contempt for the material world was nothing more than an exaggerated version of "Lay up not for yourselves treasures on earth, where moth and rust do corrupt...but in heaven, where neither moth nor rust corrupt" (Matt. 6:19-20).

Their narrow idea of a saving Gnosis ("knowledge") was somewhat more complex. To begin with, it was a one-sided exaggeration of Christ's promise, "Ye shall know the truth and the truth shall make you free" (John 8:32). But it was also an extension of the distinctly Johannine notion that Christ's death and Resurrection were not so much a sacrifice in the Jewish cult-sense, as a demonstration of heavenly power ("No man taketh my life from me, but I have power to lay it down, and I have power to take it up again"; 10:18). The crucifixion and Resurrection were there-fore described as a "glorification", i.e. the making visible of Christ's doxa, his celestial "radiance" and "potency" (7:39; 13:31; 21:19; etc.).

Paul, on the other hand, whose Pharisaic background never deserted him, saw them chiefly as the transformation of the sacrificial cult into the corporate crucifixion of mortality, and the resulting spiritual freedom in Christ (Rom. 6:2ff; Gal. 5:24f; etc.).

But the Gnostics, who especially hated the Jews, avoided traditional references to Jesus as a "sacrifice" (e.g. John 1:19). For them, his spiritual gifts allowed him simply to break through the powers that bind us to the elements (Gal. 4:9; Eph. 1:20ff; Phil, 2:10-

11; Col. 2:15; etc.), reminding us at the same time of our heavenly origin and destiny. Having thus "opened the way", he is able to draw us back to the Light (John 3:19-21; 12132). Those who refuse the invitation condemn themselves (3:18).

This, according to the Gnostics, was the true interpretation of the NT, and the meaning of the saving Gnosis which Jesus imparted to his disciples.

Gnosticism, then, "looks like a special way of viewing materials which are largely Christian in origin" (italics added; Wilson, Gospel of Philip, 17).

We must, of course, be wary of ignoring--as the Gnostics sometimes did--the enormous heritage of "normative" Judaism in the Church. Apocalyptic never made this error; it was always bound securely to the expectations of the OT which it interpreted with the visionary insight of men who suddenly appreciated the transcendent nature of the coming eschaton.

But if we make the necessary allowances for the Gnostic's "special way" of viewing things, we may use the newly recovered "materials that are largely Christian in origin" to help us determine just what the early Church actually taught. This is what responsible scholars have been doing for some years now, working back from the flood of new documents to the original ideas held by the Church. The opposite is true of the pre-Christian sources, from which one can look forward into the heart of apocalyptic Christianity.

The result is that the "great void" which once existed in our knowledge of the intertestamental and early Christian periods has been largely repaired.

"The breakthrough came when, in the years following 1946, this void was at least partly filled by the almost simultaneous discovery of the Dead Sea Scrolls and of the twelve volumes of Gnostic texts from Nag Hammadi...Since these texts became available the whole picture of the world of the Early Church has changed" (Danielou, Theology of Jewish Christianity, 3).

Thanks to these discoveries, we now see "how marvelously it has become possible in the last ten years, after seventeen centuries of obscurity, to begin *to discern once again the features of the unknown face of the Primitive Church*" (italics added; ibid., 5. Written in 1964).

And what is it that we discern?

"The traditions of the Elders, to which Papias, Irenaeus and Clement of Alexandria refer, and which they claim to have come down to them from Apostolic times, though *distinguishing them from the Rule of Faith*; there is the 'gnosis of the mysteries' into which the author of the *Epistle of Barnabas* proposes to initiate the *more advanced* Christians; and there are the special teachings which purport to have been given *in private* by Christ to his followers after the Resurrection, and to have been preserved in oral tradition" (italics added; ibid., 3)

Some of these early "features of the unknown face of the Primitive Church" are "apt to appear strange and distorted" to modern readers. Nevertheless, they were "the dominant Jewish thought-forms of the time, namely apocalyptic". Unfortunately they were in the past "all too cavalierly glossed over in search for conventional formulas" (ibid., 4).

These *original* Christian thought-forms were "conceived in terms of revelation of cosmic secrets of the dwelling places of angels and demons and the *souls of men*; of the secrets of history written before hand in the book of God; of the mystery of the Cross of Glory" (the law of sacrifice), "and the *pre-existent Church*, at once old and yet young and beautiful. The heart of its faith is the affirmation that Christ alone has *penetrated beyond the veil,* and opened the seals of the heavenly scroll, achieving Paradise for those who bear the Name of the Son of God" (italics added; ibid., 4).

But even while recounting what the Primitive Church actually believed, Father Danielou--a Cardinal in the Catholic Church--shows that he too suffers occasionally from the disease of "orthodoxy" that plagued Father Beumer, Hamerton-Kelly and Pastor Kasemann, In short, the devout believer discovers again that he cannot accept as a matter of present faith what the scholar has so painstakingly recovered from out of the past.

"This theology", he begins to rationalize, "suffered from serious limitations in its terminology and in some of its conclusions, and these defects exposed it to heresy and misinterpretations which vitiated its usefulness as a vehicle of salvation, and led to its supercession by a more adequate instrument" (italics added; ibid., 4).

The original theology of the Church, we are thus led to believe, was inadequate for saving souls, and had to be replaced by a more "modern" version!!

A better description of the "Great Apostasy" we have never read.

Even so, Danielou believes that it would be "useful" for us to reconstruct this very "earliest Christian theology", because it was "*a tradition still in living contact with the world of Scripture*" (italics added; ibid., 4, 5).

Traditional histories of theology, on the other hand, trace the development of Christian dogma "by the steady increase in the *infiltration of Greek philosophical terms and concepts.* Harnack, for example, regarded theology as born from the *union of Gospel message and Greek philosophy*; and in his *History of Dogma* a Jewish Christian theology finds no place, simply because he *never suspected its existence*" (italics added; ibid., 2).

Here, again, the true scholar takes over, telling us what the Latter Day Saints have always taught: that "orthodoxy" consists of "the philosophies of men mingled with Scripture"!

Thanks to the increasing knowledge of the "face of the Primitive Church", even Vatican councils have begun to demand that the Community of Faith return to Biblical Christianity and to the practices of the original Christians. Many Protestants have also begun to consider once again the "gifts of the Spirit", apostleship, prophecy, "laying on of hands", baptism by immersion, anointing of the sick with holy oil, etc. And though others of the Church's original teachings still seem unpalatable to modern "orthodoxy", they must likewise be courageously accepted if Christianity is to possess what the Savior's own circle of disciples taught and believed.

Sadly enough, however, the present trend is away from belief, and the fault lies largely in the feeble, watered-down "piety" served to the average "Sunday-go-to-meeting" congregations of "orthodox" sects. Such churches are becoming mere social clubs, devoid of literal significance, and bereft of credible authority with which to bless their members. Consequently, as Paul prophesied centuries ago, they "have a form of godliness, but deny the power thereof"; 2 Tim. 315).

Their young and old are increasingly atheistic, for they can no longer believe that merely "accepting Jesus" will save them from eternal death. Neither does it content them to be promised a mysterious "pie-in-the-sky", whose very nature or purpose remains undefined. Mere sentiment and morality constitute the whole of their bland diet; the most it can offer by way of religious experience is to "be kind to one's neighbor"--an activity that even unbelievers can fully share.

Science is slowly but surely demolishing the faith of such religions. They are terrified to learn that the things Jesus taught were already taught by others be-fore him. Worse still, "uncouth" religious doctrines abhorred by "orthodoxy" turn out to have been accepted by the earliest ancestors of the "chosen people"--including polytheism, man's inherent divinity, and the holiness of sexuality.

"Orthodoxy" thus faces considerable of a dilemma: did the early religion of Israel come from God, or did it simply evolve, as skeptics affirm?

If it came from God, why did he not give the truth to his earliest children? Why did he wait until the time of Christ to reveal himself fully? Why did the Patriarchs and the ancestral Hebrews (not to mention the rest of mankind) have so different a religion from the one which "orthodoxy" says came to the Jews at the "meridian of time"?

Or, if it evolved from this more "primitive" ancestral religion, then where is the authority it claims to possess? If it was not given by God, but simply developed out of old superstition, then why pay it heed? Interesting it might be, but certainly devoid of supernatural power.

Whatever the answer to these questions, we must begin to take into account what history reveals, as well as what faith asserts. "Orthodoxy", unfortunately, is ill-prepared to accept the results of such a broad program.

Mormonism, on the other hand, is fully able to reconcile both history and faith, both the old and the new, It boldly announces that the Gospel existed before the world was, and will continue throughout numberless new worlds. It is the same Gospel which was taught to Adam and the Patriarchs, and to the Primitive Church, as the new document finds are demonstrating. Its fragments are found nearly every-where every detail of its basic truths can be found in some ancient source or other, often with the historic connections still showing. With this Eternal Gospel history has no argument.

Mormonism contains the fullest account of the Eternal Gospel anywhere. "Or-thodoxy", limited to the moral teachings of the public canon, has eliminated most of its vitality, because it has lost all connections between man and the Cosmos, making God "totally other", separating Creation from Creator by an "unbridgeable gulf". What "has no root" indeed has no future. Man is thus reduced to pathetic i contingency, simply to flatter the "majesty" of God.

The greatest number of the world's early religions, however--including the ancestral religion of the Semites--taught the divine nature of intelligence, and man's essential kinship to God, for in the Eternal Gospel, like always comes from like, Even in the East, the highest truth was tat tvam asi, "that thou art", referring to the divine spark of God in every man, and the unbroken continuity of all things with their Source (Svetasvatara Upanishad). There never was a Creation "out of nothing", or a "magic" beginning by divine fiat.

The Eternal Gospel is a religion with a comprehensive plan, "Orthodoxy", by contrast, has been likened to a play with only a second act. The spectator arrives in the middle, not knowing of anything that went before, or what is to follow. He has no inkling of any direction or true purpose to the drama. His belief lacks the "grand scheme" which gives all genuine philosophies their meaning.

Mormonism supplies the beginning to this play, and explains very concretely what the end will be. Man's destiny is thereby illuminated, for he knows, like the Christian of old, that he is a "son of the Living Father", and that his goal is to share in the sacred work of Creation. God's greatest desire is to lift him to the full image of divinity, to enable him to perpetuate life in an endlessly expanding universe. To this, there was no beginning, and will be no end.

It is most remarkable that Joseph Smith was able to reconstruct such a religion in the early days of frontier America. As we indicated at the beginning, this was all the more surprising since no one else in modern times had ever discussed its possibility, or the chance that lost records from the early Church would one day pour forth to verify or disprove the unusual claims.

Yet we now see how amazingly accurate his intuition was.

Consider, for example, his reconstruction of the Christian Temple experience-- previously unsuspected by one and all.

The general scheme, he proposed, was patterned after Israel's wandering in the "lone and dreary" wilderness in search of covenants and laws that would enable them to enter into the presence of God. This he might have deduced from a careful reading of Hebrews. But that early Christians had actually penetrated through the veil of the Temple and participated in a "Bridal Chamber" rite, could not have been learned from any literature available to Joseph Smith, The lost writings of the Church, however, now assure us that this was the case, and that men and women were thereupon married for eternity, after the image of Christ's "marriage" to the Church.

Joseph Smith also knew that this symbolic journey was restricted to those holding the Melchizedek Priesthood (Gospel of Philip, Saying 125). "Orthodoxy" assumes that every Christian is automatically a member of this priesthood, yet the text shows clearly that only "some" were ("if some are of the tribe of the priesthood"; compare also Heb. 7:5-17). Heracleon, an early 2nd century exegete, who also limited the Holy of Holies to the pneumatics, or bearers of the highest priesthood, shows that the outer precincts of the

Temple were still associated with the Levites, or Aaronic Priesthood, exactly as in Mormon Temples (Wilson, Gospel of Philip, 141), There it was that baptisms were carried out (Gospel of Philip, Saying 76), just as in Mormon practice, But behind the veil--where the symbolic "Face" or "Presence" of the Lord resided--the initiate "received the Light" (Saying 127), for he had to do it in this world for the "other place" (ibid.).

Much more could be written about such correspondences between Joseph Smith's version of the Temple and ancient temple-worship, but these lie outside of our present task.

The Dead Sea Scrolls and Nag Hammadi texts meanwhile provide material enough to test the remarkable parallels between Mormonism and the Eternal Gospel, including the "three degrees of glory", prophecy and revelation, the pre-existence of man, the Heavenly Mother, the Council in Heaven, God's special name of "Man", Eternal Marriage, Christ's preaching in the spirit-world, procreation after the Resurrection, man's divine origin and destiny, and the tradition of "esoteric" teaching, To these could be added baptism for the dead, the structure of the Temple cult, "secret" prayer-circles, dispensationalism, cosmism, and many other features of present-day Mormonism.

All of these occur repeatedly in the texts we have discussed, The mere fact that one-sided exegesis by the Gnostics sometimes altered them in eccentric ways does not in the slightest reduce their significance, It has always been the task of scholars to search out the original sources behind historical phenomena, and this is presently what is required of the student who approaches the material lying before us.

Ms. Layton's criticism of Erickson's parallels between the "Garden of Eden" scene in the Hypostasis of the Archons and the L.D.S. Temple Endowment (p, 10ff) is a good example of the failure to heed this advice. She is intentionally misleading because she searches only for myopic dissimilarities that could be invoked to camouflage the basic connections between the two. But the confused order of events in the Gnostic text is of little consequence when we consider that both accounts are clearly based on the same original source, i.e. the Garden-scene in Genesis. Furthermore, the presence of an "Instructor" in both instances shows that a teaching situation has been created out of the Biblical story; and one who knows the Gnostics will quickly recognize that they traditionally represented Satan as a "tool" of the Holy Spirit (fem. gender), just as the Latter Day Saint Endowment makes him a "tool" in God's plan to bring knowledge to Adam and Eve. (See Gospel of Philip, Saying 16: "The archons thought it was by their own power and will that they were doing what they did, but the Holy Spirit in secret was contriving everything through them as it wished.")

The casual reader, however, is entitled to omit this kind of historical analysis, and to simply note the presence of "Mormon" ideas wherever he finds them. If he discovers--as did Ms. Layton's correspondent--that the ancient texts are full of "striking similarities" to Joseph Smith's teachings, let him simply explain how they came to be there, and how the Mormon prophet could have foretold their existence in such a remarkable fashion. For they are indeed there, whatever one's "evaluation" of them; this in itself demands explanation.

It should be stressed that Mormons also accept the canonical Scriptures as the word of God, though they have been robbed of "many parts that are plain and most precious; and also many covenants of the Lord have they taken away" (1 Nephi 13:26).

The (OT, especially, shows signs of extensive tampering and editing, only the latest of which was the so-called "Deuteronomic Revision" (ca. 620--400 B.C.). It also suffers from enforced assimilation of traditions inherited from both Yahwism and pre-Mosaic Israel. Mormonism reads these jumbled records quite easily because it recognizes the nature of the changes that occurred after the experience at Mt. Sinai, when the original Law was superseded by a lesser Law (Joseph Smith Version of the Bible, Ex. 34:1-2).

This has been fully verified by apocryphal accounts which describe two sets of Torah given at the time of Sinai (e.g. 4 Ezra 14:4-6). According to recent scholars, true knowledge had been communicated to all the Patriarchs, including Moses. This first Law "emanated from the Tree of Life; but...Israel by worshipping the golden calf was judged unworthy of benefitting from (it). Therefore, Moses, following the divine command, gave the people other Tables which came from the side of the Tree of Good and Evil...The first Tables...were the source of eternal life on earth. The second Tables represented the indirect or 'fragmented' manifestation of this light" (Leo Schaya, op. cit., 15-16). Thus, "the old religion and the Mosaic religion were historically distinct" (Vriezen, op. cit., 227).

The books which were finally accepted into the NT canon are generally complete as they stand; but it is obvious from the witness of history that they too fail to discuss many of the Church's original teachings and practices. Mormons nevertheless read what is left very literally.

When the texts describe man's pre-existence, for example, or the natural father-hood of God, we accept them just as they are. The same is true of statements that men will someday be changed into the very "image of the Lord" to participate in the "divine nature" (2 Pet. 1:4), or that Savior and Saved are of "one origin", being truly "brethren" and "joint heirs" in the Kingdom of God.

The NT is distinguished for its inspired call to Christ, a fact which explains its perennial appeal and its exalted place in Mormon Scripture. Like the Book of Mormon, it contains the "good news" of the Gospel, and the witness that Jesus is the Christ, and man's power unto salvation.

Both, however, remain silent about teachings and ordinances beyond baptism--a limitation which history now affirms, and "orthodoxy" can no longer deny: "Baptism is the holy house, redemption is the holy of the holy one, but the Holy of Holies is the Bridal Chamber. Baptism has the resurrection, and the redemption is to hasten into the Bridal Chamber. But the Bridal Chamber is superior to the others..." (Gospel of Philip, Saying 76).

It is this writer's opinion that the Primitive Church remained very small, being limited to the immediate circle of the disciples and apostles. As it spread into the world, it became exclusively dependent upon the public canon of teachings, and eventually was replaced--as Father Danielou admits--by the so-called "Great Church" of the West.

Even the Reformation recognized such changes, but since it lacked historical knowledge of the primitive epoch, it could never return to the Church's true origins.

Nevertheless, even Mormons believe that the leaders of the Reformation were inspired to lay the groundwork for eventual restoration of the Primitive Gospel. In fact, it is the conviction of Latter Day Saints that men everywhere have received as much of the Truth as they are ready to practice (2 Nephi 29:7-14). And because of God's justice, those who presently lack knowledge will have opportunity to be-come "heirs of the kingdom" at some future time. This is the eminently reasonable doctrine of Mormonism, which thus affirms the fairness of God's plan for all.

Meanwhile, the rediscovery of so much material from early Christians and Jews helps us to substantiate what they actually taught and believed. It would be best to consider the picture in its entirety, to identify the various movements and "trajectories" that composed it, and to learn how they shifted from generation to generation, always in a state of flux.

Those who have enjoyed Einar Erickson's more direct presentation of isolated parallels should continue to do so, assured that he correctly reaches the "bottom line"--the net result--of such studies, even though the connecting arguments may often be lacking. Indeed, very few have been able to convey with such spiritual conviction the fact that the Dead Sea Scrolls and the Nag Hammadi texts do testify strongly of "Mormon" ideas in the milieu of the early Church.

If Ms. Layton was once impressed by Erickson's talks, let her reconsider the true significance of what he discusses. All scholars today recognize that the new discoveries were connected in very intimate ways with Primitive Christianity. They were in fact much closer to the central core of original belief than the 3rd and 4th century amalgam of Greek metaphysics and Canon which came to be known as "orthodoxy". Ms. Layton will never be able to wish away this ultimate fact, either by denying its existence, or by failure to understand the historical processes which constituted it.

BIBLIOGRAPHY OF MODERN SOURCES

Abbreviations:

FSAC--From the Stone Age to Christianity (William Albright).

JBL--Journal of Biblical Literature

YGC--Yahweh and the Gods of Canaan (William Albright).

Aistleitner, J., Wörterbuch der ugaritischen Sprache, Leipzig, 1965.

Albright, William F., "Archaic Survivals in the Text of Canticles", Hebrew and Semitic Studies, ed. D.W. Thomas and W.D. McHardy, Oxford, 1963.

From the Stone Age to Christianity (FSAC), N.Y., 1957.

Yahweh and the Gods of Canaan (YGC), N.Y., 1968.

Allegro, John, "The Untold Story of the Scrolls", Harper's 233 (Aug. 1966), 46ff,

Baer, Richard, Jr., Philo's Use of the Categories Male and Female, Leiden, 1970,

Barth, Markus, Anchor Bible, Ephesians, N.Y., 1974.

Batey, R.A., "Jewish Gnosticism and the 'Hieros Gamos' of Eph V:21-33", New Testament Studies 16 (1963-4), 121-7.

Bauer, Walter, Rechtglaubigkeit und Ketzerei im altesten Christentum (English translation: Orthodoxy and Heresy in Earliest Christianity, Philadelphia, 1971).

Bauer-Arndt-Gingrich, A Greek-English Lexicon of the New Testament, Chicago, 1957.

Beumer, Johannes, "Die altchristliche Idee einer praexistierenden Kirche", Wissenschaft und Wahrheit 9 (1942), 13-22.

Bianchi, Ugo, (editor), Le Origini dello Gnosticismo, Leiden, 1967.

Brooks, Beatrice, "Fertility Cult Functionaries in the OT", Journal of Biblical Literature 66 (1941), 227-53.

Brown, Raymond E., Anchor Bible, John, N.Y., 1966.

The Semitic Background of the Term "Mystery" in the NT, Philadelphia, 1968.

Speech, at Provo, Utah, May 7, 1974.

Brownlee, Wm. H., in Biblical Archaeologist, Sept. 1960.

Buchanan, Geo. Wesley, Anchor Bible, Hebrews, N.Y., 1972.

Charles, R,H ,, Book of Enoch, London, 1913.

Charlesworth, James H ,, "The Odes of Solomon--Not Gnostic", Catholic Biblical Quarterly 31 (1969), 357-69.

Cross, Frank M., Jr., The Ancient Library of Qumran and Modern Biblical Studies, N.Y., 1968.

Cumont, Franz, Astrology and Religion Among the Greeks and Romans, reprint, N.Y., 1960.

Oriental Religion in Roman Paganism, reprint, N.Y., 1956.

Danielou, Jean, Les Manuscrits de la Mer Morte et les Origins du Christianisme, Paris, 1957.

The Theology of Jewish Christianity, Engl. Transl., London, 1964.

Dummelow, J.R., The One Volume Bible Commentary, N.Y., 1966.

Dupont-Sommers, A., The Essene Writings from Qumran, Oxford, 1961.

Eichrodt, Walter, Theology of the Old Testament, Engl. transl., Philadelphia, 1961.

Eissfeldt, Otto, "El and Yahweh", Journal of Semitic Studies 1(1956), 25-37.

Eliade, Mircea, The Myth of the Eternal Return, Princeton, 1954.

Emerton, J,A., "The Origin of the Son of Man Imagery", Journal of Theological Studies 9 (1958), 225-42.

Ford, Massyngberde, "'The Son of Man'--A Euphemism?", Journal of Biblical Literature 87, 257-66.

Freed, Edwin, "The Son of Man and the Fourth Gospel", Journal of Biblical Literature 86, 462-9.

Gartner, Bertil, The Temple and the Community in Qumran, Cambridge, 1965.

Caster, T,H., The Dead Sea Scriptures, N.Y., 1956 and 1976 editions,

Ginzberg, Louis, Legends of the Jews, Philadelphia, 1909-38.

Goodenough, Erwin R., By Light, Light!, New Haven, 1935.

Gordon, Cyrus, Before Columbus, N.Y., 1973 edition, addendum.

Grant, Robert M., The Early Christian Doctrine of God, University of Virginia. 1966.

Gnosticism and Early Christianity, N.Y., 1959.

"The Mystery of Marriage in the Gospel of Philip", Vigiliae Christianae 15 (1961), 129-40.

Graves, Robert, and Patai, Raphael, Hebrew Myths, N.Y., 1966.

Grobel, Kendrick, The Gospel of Truth, Nashville, 1960.

Hamerton-Kelly, R,G., Pre-Existence, Wisdom and the Son of Man, Cambridge, 1973,

von Harnack, Adolph, History of Dogma, reprint, N.Y., 1961.

Harris, Bendel, Fragments of Philo Judaeus, Cambridge, 1886.

Harrison, R.K., The Dead Sea Scrolls, N.Y., 1961.

Hasel, Gerhard, New Testament Theology: Basic Issues in the Current Debate, Grand Rapids, 1978.

Old Testament Theology: Basic Issues in the Current Debate, Grand Rapids, 1972.

Hastings, ed., Dictionary of the Bible, N.Y., 1903.

Dictionary of the Bible, N.Y., 1963.

Encyclopedia of Religion and Ethics

Heidel, Alexander, The Babylonian Genesis, Chicago, 1937.

Helmbold, Andrew, The Nag Hammadi Texts and the Bible, Grand Rapids, 1967.

Herdner, A., Corpus des tablettes en cuneiforme alphabetique, Paris, 1963.

Hofner Maria, Die vorislamitischen Religionen Arabiens, Stuttgart, 1970.

Hooke, S H., The Siege Perilous, London, 1956.

Interpreter's Bible, Nashville, 1952.

Interpreter's Dictionary of the Bible, Nashville, 1962, Supplementary volume, 1976,

Isenberg, Wesley; see Robinson, James M., The Nag Hammadi Library.

James, E.O., The Cult of the Mother Goddess, N.Y., 1959.

Jewish Encyclopedia, N.Y., 1905.

Kasemann, Ernst, Das wandernde Gottesvolk, Gottingen, 1961.

Koester, Helmut, and Robinson, James, M., Trajectories Through Early Christianity, Philadelphia, 1971.

Kramer, S.N., The Sacred Marriage Rite, Indiana University, 1969.

Layton, Helaine, The Truth About the Dead Sea Scrolls and Nag Hammadi Writings in Reference to Mormonism, Wheeling, Ill., 1979.

MacRae, George, "Gnosticism and New Testament Studies", Bible Today 38 (1968), 2623-30.

"The Jewish Background of the Gnostic Sophia Myth", Novum Testamentum 12 (1970), 86-101.

May, Herbert G., "The Patriarchal Idea of God", Journal of Biblical Studies 60 (1944), 113-28.

Milgrom, Jacob, "The Temple Scroll", Biblical Archaeologist 41 (1978), 105-20.

Morgenstern, Julian, "The Divine Triad in Biblical Mythology", Journal of Biblical Literature 64 (1945), 15-37.

"The Gates of Righteousness", Hebrew Union College Annual, 1927, 1-37.

Some Significant Antecedents of Christianity, Leiden, 1966.

"'Son of Man' of Daniel 7:13f", Journal of Biblical Literature 64 (1945), 65-77.

Mowry, Lucetta, The Dead Sea Scrolls and the Early Church, Notre Dame, 1966,

Nibley, Hugh, Since Cumorah, Salt Lake City, 1967.

Nielsen, Litlef, "Die Muttergöttin in Kanaan", Zeitschrift der Deutschen Morgenländischen Gesellschaft, 1938, 526-51.

"Ras Shamra Mythologie und biblische Theologie", Abhandlungenen für die
Kunde des Morgenlandes, Vol. 2, no. 4, 2.

Neumann, Erich, The Great Mother, N.Y., 1955.

New International Dictionary of New Testament Theology, The, Grand Rapids, 1975-8.

O'Brian, John, "Why Priests Marry", The Christian Century 87 (1970), 417.

Pagels, Elaine, The Gnostic Paul, Philadelphia, 1975.

The Johannine Gospel in Gnostic Exegesis, Nashville, 1973.

Patai, Raphael, The Hebrew Goddess, N.Y., 1967.

Perrin, Norman, Rediscovering the Teaching of Jesus, N.Y., 1967,

Phipps, William, Was Jesus Married?, N.Y., 1970.

Pope, Marvin, El in the Ugaritic Texts, Leiden, 1955.

Anchor Bible, Job, N.Y., 1965.

Anchor Bible, Song of Songs, N.Y., 1977.

Quesnell, Quentin, "Made Themselves Eunuchs for the Kingdom of Heaven", Catholic
Biblical Quarterly 30 (1968), 335-58.

Ringgren, Helmer, Israelite Religion, Engl. trans., Philadelphia, 1966,

Roberts, J.J.M., The Earliest Semitic Pantheon, Baltimore, 1972.

Robinson, H. Wheeler, "The Council of Yahweh", Journal of Biblical Studies, 1944, 151-
7.

Robinson, James M., The Nag Hammadi Library, N.Y., 1977.

Robinson, James M., and Helmut Koester, Trajectories Through Early Christianity,
Philadelphia, 1971.

Russell, B.S., The Method and Message of Jewish Apocalyptic, Philadelphia, 1964.

Sampley, J. Paul, For the Two Shall Become One Flesh, Cambridge, 1971.

Schaya, Leo, The Universal Meaning of the Kabbalah, London, 1971.

Schenke, H.- M., "Las Evangelium nach Phillipus", Theologische Literaturzeitung, 1959, 2-22.

Der Gott "Mensch" in der Gnosis, Gottingen, 1962.

"Nag Hamadi Studien III", Zeitschrift für Religions- und Geistesgeschichte, 1962, 352-61.

Schiele, Friedrich, "Harnack's 'Probabilia' Concerning the Address and the Author of the Epistle to the Hebrews", American Journal Of Theology 9 {1910), 290-308.

Schlier, Heinrich, Der Brief an die Epheser, Dusseldorf, 1957.

Scholem, Gershom, Major Trends in Jewish Mysticism, N.Y., 1954,

On the Kabbalah and Its Symbolism, N.Y., 1965.

"Zur Entwicklungsgeschichte der kabbalistischen Konzeption der Schechinah", Eranos Jahrbuch 21 (1952), 45-107.

Schweitzer, Albert, The Mysticism of the Apostle Paul, reprint, N.Y., 1968.

Segelberg, Eric, "The Coptic-Gnostic Gospel According to Philip", Numen, 1960, 189- . 200.

Sjoberg, E., Der Menschensohn im Athiopischen Henochbuch, Lund, 1946.

Smith, Morton, Clement of Alexandria and the Secret Gospel of Mark, Cambridge, Mass. 1973.

Stamm, Raymond T., in Interpreter's Bible, Nashville, 1953.

Stendahl, Krister, The Scrolls and the New Testament, N.Y., 1959.

Strack, Hermann, and Billerbeck, Paul, Kommentar zum Neuen Testament aus Talmud und Midrasch, Munich, 1922.

de Vaux, Roland, The Early History of Israel, Philadelphia, 1968,

Vermes, Geza, The Dead Sea Scrolls in English, Harmondsworth, 1968.

Vriezen, Theodore, The Religion of Ancient Israel, London, 1967,

Waite, A.E., The Holy Kabbalah, N.Y. reprint, 1960.

Weber, F., Jüdische Theologie, Leipzig, 1897.

Widtsoe, John A., "Temple Worship", Utah Genealogical and Historical Magazine, April, 1921.

Wilson, Edmund, The Dead Sea Scrolls, N.Y., 1969.

Wilson, R. McLain, The Gospel of Philip, London, 1962.

"Simon, Dositheus and the Dead Sea Scrolls", Zeitschrift für Religions- und Geistesgeschichte, 1957, 21-30.

Yamauchi, Edwin, Pre-Christian Gnosticism, Grand Rapids, 1973.

22660119R00045

Made in the USA
Lexington, KY
12 May 2013